<u>The</u> **Happy** Labrador

Your Guide to a **Happy**, Well-Mannered Labrador

- ➢ Keep your Labrador happy
- ➢ Raise a well-behaved Lab
- ➢ Prevent behaviour issues
- ➢ Fulfil your Lab needs
- ➢ Be the ideal guardian
- ➢ Avoid common mistakes

Asia Moore

Dog Behavior Expert & Acclaimed Author

"Labradors are miracles with paws."
— Unknown

Preface

It takes time, commitment, tenacity, consistency and knowledge to raise a happy and healthy Labrador that doesn't suffer from health and behavioral issues.

This book is not like most other breed-specific books, because we believe that it's far better for all parties concerned (human and canine) to **prevent** problems rather than suffering the frustrations of living with or learning how to eliminate problems and rehabilitate a Lab that has already developed health or behavioral issues.

It is always better to prevent unwanted behaviors than to hope you have what it takes to eliminate them in the future, after your family is at their wits end, your neighbors hate you, your friends no longer visit and you're having guilty thoughts of re-homing every time you drive past your local SPCA.

If you want a happy, well-mannered Labrador canine companion to be an enjoyable part of your family, it absolutely matters how you raise your dog.

Every breed has uniquely different needs, because although most dogs are now companions, each breed was originally developed for the purpose of assisting humans in some specific capacity.

For instance, a Border Collie is a very smart, high-energy dog who excels at the job of sheep herding. Therefore, if you expect this dog to sit around doing nothing all day while you're at work, you will most likely return to holes in your drywall, torn apart couches and a home that looks like it's been through a cyclone.

On the other hand, the Shih Tzu lap dog, which was only permitted to be owned by royalty, sat on silk pillows and was used to warm beds, has vastly different daily exercise requirements and would be a poor choice for someone requiring a companion that could protect them from being mugged on streets ravaged by gang warfare.

Every dog breed has different talents and needs and when you decide to share your life with a particular breed, you need to also be prepared to provide your dog with what he or she needs to be a happy member of your family.

Almost all canine problems, both mentally and physically, are a direct result of ignorance or unwillingness on the part of the human guardian to choose the right dog and then learn what their dog truly needs.

This book is uniquely different, and humans reading it need to clearly understand that it is not about describing what to do to eliminate problematic canine behaviors that have already occurred.

Rather, the main focus of this breed-specific book is to describe what the human guardian needs to understand and commit to doing on a daily basis in order to match the Labrador's needs, so that they can raise a happy, healthy and well-behaved dog that never has to experience behavioral issues.

Do not expect this book to be like all the others that set out endless correlations between specific mal-behaviors and what steps or actions the human guardian can take in an attempt to correct them.

In other words, this book is a totally new slant on raising a happy and healthy Labrador, because it will focus on the prevention of behavioral issues rather than addressing them after they have already surfaced.

About the Author

Asia Moore

Dog Behavior Expert & Acclaimed Author

Ever since my first birthday, I was immersed in nature, and have always enjoyed a special connection with all creatures, great and small. I learned to communicate and "talk" with many animals in their language, both wild and domesticated. At the age of twelve, dogs started becoming the main focus of my life, when I began training and grooming my first puppy.

When friends and neighbors began to recognize how well behaved my dog was and were impressed with all the tricks and routines she could perform, often without a spoken word, they asked me to train their dogs, too.

I've been so fortunate to have experienced the unconditional love of so many dogs over the years, all of whom taught me many different life lessons. I began this journey with my first mixed breed ("Cindy") who protected me from my marauding brothers, then my mixed breed ("Pepper") who had an amazing human vocabulary and always knew when someone was not to be trusted, my Blue Heeler ("Bugsy") who would hike endless trails and swim miles with me, to my current loving Shih Tzu ("Boris") and all those in between.

Now, some 40 years later, and endless different breeds, hybrids and mutts, from tiny Chihuahuas to bouncing Belgians, many fur friends have passed through my life.

For the last 40 years, I have been running my dog whispering, dog sitting and grooming businesses and have had countless experiences of working with dogs of all breeds and their guardians. It has not always been easy, I have had my fair share of struggles and setbacks, but I have always loved and been passionate about what I do. All these years of experience taught me invaluable lessons in all aspects of the human-canine relationship and interaction. For instance, I learnt how to communicate with our canine friends, understand their needs and help them lead a fulfilling and happy life, to name a few.

Clients' dogs now remain the focal point of my dog whispering, sitting and grooming life, while I also focus on freelance writing of breed-specific books. I have so far authored over 300 books, where my goal is to pass on my knowledge and experience to all responsible dog owners (Must Have Publishing.com). At the same time, I am training human guardians, so that they can improve their relationship with their dog and understand how to prevent and alleviate behavioral issues (K-9 Super Heroes Dog Whispering.com).

As well, I have recently added an additional online branch to my business, which I call "Knows To Nose" to help humans "know" how to choose the right dog "nose" for their energy and lifestyle, before they make the wrong decision and end up with troubling problems.

I feel blessed that the canine world has been a major part of my life for so many years, as it never gets old. I continuously stay in touch with my clients through my business websites and personal consultations and I love how there is always room to learn more, because every unique dog brings new lessons to light and enhances your life in untold, indescribable ways.

I'd like to thank you for purchasing The Happy Labrador and reassure you that the pages of this book contain the distilled knowledge of over 40 years experience. When taken to heart, the knowledge, tips and techniques in this book can help you along your special journey inside the amazing world of our canine friends, so that you can know the unconditional love, special bond and joy that only our four-legged companions selflessly offer to us flawed humans.

Visit Asia online at the following locations:

www.K-9SuperHeroesDogWhispering.com
www.KnowsToNose.com
www.MustHavePublishing.com

Table of Contents

Chapter 1: Introduction to the Happy Labrador

"You can't buy Love. But you can buy a Chocolate Lab which is essentially the same thing."
— Unknown

The purpose of this book is to focus on the important steps the humans in this relationship really need to be aware of and commit to providing in order to ensure that the Lab can live a happy and healthy life, which in turn will ensure a happy relationship for everyone.

Even though humans and dogs have been relying on one another for more than 30,000 years, it's still highly important that you choose the companion that is best suited to your particular lifestyle.

Within the pages of this book you will find information to help you choose wisely by providing you with a clear understanding concerning whether or not YOU have what it takes to be the right match for raising a happy and well-mannered Labrador.

In addition, this book describes in detail what the human guardian needs to keep in mind and commit to doing on a daily basis in order to match the Labrador's needs, so that they can raise a happy, healthy and well-behaved dog that never has to experience behavioral issues.

All the information, suggestions, tips and advice given in this publication is the result of more than 40 years experience helping humans positively and effectively interact with the canine world.

If you take all that is written on these pages to heart, and regularly and consistently apply them, your Labrador will be a happy family member that will not have to suffer from any behavioral problems. In other words, the focus is placed on prevention, rather than trying to correct the issues after they have surfaced.

Every chapter of this book contains valuable information that will provide you with a solid understanding of the breed and the steps you need to take to raise a happy and well-behaved Labrador.

For instance, **Chapter 2** – *"Overview of the Happy Labrador"* will outline vital statistics, coat colors and common features, intelligence, temperament and interesting secrets and facts that may not be commonly known. In order to raise a contented Labrador, you need to have some basic knowledge of the breed to help you choose wisely and to comprehend their needs.

Chapter 3 – *"A Healthy Labrador is a Happy Lab"* is where you will find out what you need to know about medical care, safety and health issues that may affect the Labrador breed, including common diseases and viruses, allergies and canine CPR procedures that could save a life. Needless to say, that if your Lab is not physically healthy, he or she will not be a happy canine companion for very long, because suffering from health-related issues will undoubtedly create a miserable and ill-mannered dog.

In **Chapter 4** – *"Let Your Dog BE a Happy Dog"*, you will find information about how to let your Lab actually BE a dog, rather than attempting to turn them into a fur human, which can make for a very unhappy and ill-mannered canine.

Chapter 5 – *"Every Happy Labrador Wants Exercise"*, first outlines some of the original history of this breed; if you know what they were bred to do, you will better understand how important it is to commit to the daily exercise routines recommended in this book, without which the Labrador will not be happy for very long.

Chapter 6 – *"Feeding the Happy Labrador"*, is where you will find information about the structure of the canine jaw, various food options and feeding suggestions as well as treats to avoid for raising a happy and healthy Labrador.

In **Chapter 7** – *"Care of the Happy Labrador"*, you will find travel safety tips, licensing, insurance, grooming procedures and important care of nails, ears, teeth and paws, all of which will help you to raise a happy Labrador. This information might seem generic, but imagine going for months without washing your hair, cutting your nails or brushing your teeth. That is the reality for many dogs, because their owners have not been advised on the importance of good grooming. How happy and well-behaved do you think such an ill-cared for Lab would be?

Chapter 8 – *"Are YOU the Ideal Happy Labrador Guardian?"* is concerned with asking yourself some serious questions, including whether your energy, activity, commitment and lifestyle matches that of what the Labrador needs to be happy and well behaved. It is vital for you to give serious consideration in these questions when considering the Labrador breed, because should you choose the wrong dog to share your life with, everybody will be miserable.

Chapter 9 – *"Humans Make a LOT of Stupid Mistakes"* outlines that far too often we humans, without even realizing it, are the cause of creating behavioral problems in our canine companions. You will find out what are the common mistakes to avoid (and the right thing to do!) when it comes to socialization, accidental rewards, fear of noises, the right collars, basic rules and boundaries, adolescent craziness and more. Simply being aware of the many mistakes we humans can often inadvertently be guilty of when raising our canine companions, can mean the difference between a Happy Labrador with no behavioral issues or a life of frustration and correction.

Chapter 10 – *"Happy Labrador Body Language"*, outlines the basics of learning Labrador body language, and will help you be safe around other dogs. Learning to properly "read" a dog's intentions can prevent an unwanted encounter with another canine, and this will help to ensure that everyone remains happy.

In Chapter 11 – *"Training Basics for a Happy Labrador"* you will learn valuable training tips and routines that will help to keep your Lab truly happy and well behaved for their entire life. It's no surprise that a properly trained Labrador will be a much happier companion that everyone enjoys being around, and will be far less likely to develop behaviour issues later in life. Developing a basic training program and learning to teach your Lab commands and discipline is all part of starting your dog off on the right paw.

Chapter 12 – *"What If You Slip Up?"* is only necessary because we humans tend to get too busy and overwhelmed with the rigors of daily living, which means we sometimes forget to be consistent with providing what our Lab may need to be happy. If you slip up, this chapter has outlined a few of the more common behavioral issues and how to get yourself back on track.

Take heed humans, because when you honestly assess your own compatibility, lifestyle and energy level for being the right guardian for the Labrador, and are vigilant about following the advice and tips outlined in the following pages, you can raise a healthy and happy Labrador that will be a joy to live with and will never suffer from any behavioral issues.

Chapter 2: Overview of the Happy Labrador

I will love you forever!

"If you don't own a dog, at least one,
there is not necessarily anything wrong with you,
but there may be something wrong with your life."
— Roger A. Caras

I cannot stress enough how important it is that you understand the basics of any breed, such as size, energy level, intelligence and temperament, so that you can truly understand if you are the right person or family for a particular dog. In order to raise a happy Labrador, you need to have some basic knowledge to help you choose wisely and to ensure that your lifestyle and daily routine can meet the Lab needs.

For instance, you need to know that the bouncy and enthusiastic Labrador is an intelligent and highly energetic, purebred retriever/gun dog that is a member of the Working Dog category and thus needs plenty of vigorous physical exercise on a daily basis.

You also need to keep in mind that the Labrador is a highly intelligent dog that will require a great deal of daily mental stimulation to keep them happy and mentally fit.

Generally speaking, while the coat color, size and temperament of the Labrador will largely depend upon the appearance and size of both breeding parents, this will be a medium to large-sized, prized sporting and hunting dog that requires plenty of your time for exercise, training, play and mental stimulation. The main overview of the breed is outlined below and is the foundation of choosing a Lab wisely and raising a happy and well-behaved dog.

Vital Statistics

While every dog is unique, there are standards that are common to each purebred canine, such as height, weight and various coat colors and features. You can also get a pretty good idea of what the puppies will look like when full grown, when you see their parents.

Height and Weight

When measured at the shoulder, the Labrador may stand between 21.5 and 24.5 inches (55 and 62 centimeters) and weigh between 55 and 80 pounds (25 and 36 kilograms) or more, depending on the size of both breed parents.

Coat Colors and Common Features

The Labrador has a double waterproof coat that is short and straight and consists of an outer layer of longer hairs and a soft, downy undercoat as an insulating layer against the cold, that holds heat and prevents cold water from penetrating the skin.

While the dog's natural oils in this dog's coat help to repel water, making the coat essentially waterproof, they also give the dog a distinctly *"doggy"* smell.

The Lab's short, flat, dense coat has a coarse feel to the touch and will be low maintenance (except twice yearly when they shed heavily), with standard coat colors including black, chocolate and yellow.

Eyes will be medium-sized, triangular-shaped and brown (in black and yellow-coated dogs) and brown or hazel (in chocolate-coated dogs) with a kind and intelligent expression, and ears will be short, pendant and triangular-shaped with rounded tips.

This breed is known for his or her thick and muscular *"otter tail"*, which helps them when swimming and can clear the contents of a coffee table with one enthusiastic wag.

How Smart is the Labrador?

While every dog is surprisingly different, despite what some "experts" might have to say about it, you need to keep in mind that there are *"people smarts"* and *"dog smarts"* and that these two ways of rating intelligence are often widely divergent or in conflict with one another.

If you really want to rate your Lab's intelligence based on what we humans think is *"smart",* there is a book *("The Intelligence of Dogs")* written in 1994 by Stanley Coren, that has become the standard for rating the particular intelligence of different canine breeds.

While I can agree, in part, with some of the information contained in this book, I can also disagree, because of personal experience, because I have found that some dogs that are rated very low on the intelligence scale are also very smart.

Therefore, I caution you not to pre-handicap your dog's level of intelligence just because of something you may have read in a well-respected book, because each dog has their own unique set of talents and much of how they develop is up to their guardian.

Coren judges canine intelligence of particular purebred canines based on three categories, as follows:

*"**Instinctive Intelligence** – a dog's ability to carry out tasks it was bred to perform, such as guarding, herding, hunting, pointing, retrieving or supplying companionship."*

*"**Adaptive Intelligence** – how well a dog is able to solve problems on its own."*

*"**Working/Obedience Intelligence** – how quickly a dog is able to learn from humans."*

In the case of the Labrador, Coren rightfully places this dog in the *"Brightest Dogs"* category, which means that they are highly intelligent, with the ability to understand new commands after fewer than 5 repetitions, and when properly trained, they have the ability to obey first commands 95% of the time, or better.

Please keep in mind that there are always exceptions to every study and a particular breed's degree of intelligence is often related to their early upbringing and how they are trained.

There is no doubt that the Labrador is a highly intelligent dog that will require a great deal of daily mental stimulation (as well as vigorous physical exercise) to keep them happy and mentally fit.

Temperament of the Labrador

As a puppy, the friendly Labrador with be a bouncy, fun-loving, affectionate, and often clumsy playmate that will knock over everything nearby. He or she will grow into a highly intelligent, strong and happy companion that is always ready for adventure and their next outdoor outing, and may still act like a bull in a china shop well into their old age.

This puppy will grow into a sweet-natured and outgoing companion that will be an energetic, happy dog with great stamina that lives to run, hunt, retrieve and play.

This is a highly versatile dog that will retain its enthusiasm for fun and adventure throughout its life and with endless stamina and energy, they will excel at a wide variety of canine sports or as a service or therapy dog, and will greet any sort of action that comes their way with great enthusiasm.

This dog will be an enthusiastic friend to everyone, which means that human and canine visitors and strangers alike will be greeted with much vigorous bouncing and tail wagging.

I used to know a Labrador, named "Stanley", that was so out of control with enthusiasm when humans came to visit that he would literally bowl you over in his excitement to greet you.

I do not recommend that you ever allow your Lab to become this out of control, because it's just too easy for a dog of this size to inadvertently hurt someone, especially a smaller child or an unstable senior.

This friendly, high-spirited, water-loving breed is the most popular purebred family dog in both North America and the United Kingdom.

Prized as sporting and hunting/retrieving gun dogs, many countries also favor the strongly built, good-natured, eager to please and easily trained Labrador as an assistance dog to aid those with disabilities or for detection work with government agencies.

This highly versatile and well-loved breed has both the energy and physical attributes to effectively hunt waterfowl or upland game for long hours under difficult conditions, as well as the ability to win awards in the show ring.

While the Labrador is an extremely enthusiastic, intelligent, easy-to-train dog with a large personality (and even larger appetite), they are also gentle around children and older people.

When combined with their naturally active nature, this furry companion will require plenty of physical exercise to prevent them from becoming obese. This will involve continued physical stimulation, involving long walks, runs or swimming, as well as games and other types of training so that they do not become bored and develop unwanted behaviors, such as chewing anything they can get their teeth on.

When you share your life with a working breed of dog that is highly intelligent and has a natural propensity to excel as a working retriever, in order for them to remain both physically and mentally healthy and happy, it is <u>absolutely vital</u> that you put in the daily effort and considerable time to begin socialization and training at an early age and continue it throughout their life.

When you take the time, you will help to ensure that your puppy grows up to be a sensible and calm adult dog that will take their cues from you, rather than acting on their own in situations that could become serious.

All guardians need to be fully aware that any dog (even one that is naturally friendly to all) that does not receive early and continual socialization throughout their lifetime may learn to become aggressive when he or she encounters people, unknown dogs and other animals, visiting neighborhood children, friends or unfamiliar situations.

Most likely, the first thing you will want to teach your Lab will be to keep their exuberance under control, so that they do not knock over children or unstable seniors in their happiness to enthusiastically greet everyone.

Also, keep in mind that the Labrador is a highly intelligent, energetic, loyal dog that is very attached to their family and easily bored.

This muscular and highly athletic dog, if given enough time and left alone in a yard, has the smarts to work its way out of a confining situation, and certainly the will to gain their freedom, including the ability to scale very high fences.

Happy Labrador Secrets

This purebred dog is named after the Labrador Sea off the Canadian coast of Newfoundland, because this is where they were originally used as retrievers.

The Labrador is also known as the *"Labrador Retriever" or simply as the "Lab"*.

Until the year 1892, all Labradors had black coats and a dog named *"Ben of Hyde"* was the first yellow Labrador to be born (in 1899).

The Labrador is the most popular dog in many countries, including Australia, Canada, New Zealand, the United Kingdom and the United States.

Labradors love everyone and are considered to be the *"happiest"* dogs on earth.

The Labrador has webbed toes and an otter tail for superior swimming.

The Labrador has a superior sense of smell and is often employed as a search and rescue, assistance dog or bomb or contraband sniffer.

The Labrador has a voracious appetite and will easily become overweight, if not given a great deal of daily exercise.

Many historians believe that two dogs, named *"Avon"* and *"Ned"*, from the Duke of Buccleuch's breeding line, are the ancestors of all modern Labradors.

The Labrador was first imported to the United States during the First World War, where this dog quickly became very popular.

The Labrador Retriever Club of Great Britain was instrumental in ensuring that the original purpose of this hunting breed was preserved, and to this end, the Club requires all Labs to earn a Working Certificate for fieldwork before they can be considered for any show competitions.

One of *the* most popular breeds of dogs worldwide, and highly valued as both a hunting companion and a service dog (according to 2019 American Kennel Club registrations), the Labrador has held the #1 popularity position amongst the 194 registered breeds since 1991.

The American Kennel Club (AKC) officially recognized the friendly, high spirited and patient Labrador in 1917, followed by United Kennel Club (UKC) recognition in 1947.

In a Nutshell

Familiarizing yourself with the Labrador's size, weight, early history and special attributes, plus understanding their intelligence level and temperament will help you to decide if this dog is the right one for you and to obtain a comprehensive understanding of the breed's needs, which is a prerequisite for raising a content and well-behaved dog.

Chapter 3: A Healthy Labrador is a Happy Lab

LABRADOR RETRIEVER

"My goal in life is to be as good a person as my dog already thinks I am."
— Unknown

If your Lab is not physically healthy, he or she will not be a happy canine companion for very long, because suffering from health-related issues can easily create a miserable and ill-mannered dog.

It's prudent that you take the many steps outlined here to help ensure that you are doing all that you can to keep on top of your Labrador's good health.

Make sure you take the time to choose a veterinarian that can provide yearly check-ups, have your dog spayed or neutered in a timely fashion, choose a healthy diet for him or her, and carefully read this section so that you educate yourself about issues that may adversely affect your dog's health.

As well, take the time to learn a little canine CPR, because doing so may save the life of your own dog, or someone else's.

Below you will find more information on each one of these steps you need to take to raise a healthy and happy Lab.

Choose your veterinarian wisely

Some clinics specialize in caring for smaller pets, while some specialize in larger animal care, and others have a wide-ranging area of expertise and will care for all animals, including livestock and reptiles.

Choosing a good veterinary clinic will be very similar to choosing the right health care clinic or doctor for your own personal health, because you want to ensure that your puppy or adult dog receives the quality care they deserve. A good place to begin your search will be by asking other dog owners where they take their furry friends and whether they are happy with the service they receive.

It's also a good idea to take your Labrador into your chosen clinic several times before they actually need to be there for any treatment, so that they are not fearful of the new smells and unfamiliar surroundings.

Consider timely neutering or spaying

There are varying opinions on the topic of the best time to neuter or spay your young Lab. One thing that most veterinarians do agree on is that earlier spaying or neutering, between 4 and 6 months of age, is a better choice than waiting longer.

Keep in mind that non-neutered or spayed males and females are more likely to display aggression related to sexual behaviour, than are dogs that have been neutered or spayed.

For instance, fighting, particularly in male dogs that is directed at other males, is less common after neutering. The intensity of other types of aggression, such as irritable aggression in females will be totally eliminated by spaying, so make that appointment at the vet's office and get it done.

Effects on General Temperament: many Lab owners often become needlessly worried that a neutered or spayed dog will lose their vigor, when in fact, many unwanted, aggressive qualities, resulting from hormonal impact, may resolve after surgery, and you will be acting as a conscientious, informed, and caring guardian.

Effects on Escape and Roaming: a neutered or spayed Lab is less likely to wander, and castrated male dogs have the tendency to patrol smaller sized outdoor areas and are less likely to participate in territorial conflicts with perceived opponents.

Possible Weight Gain: while metabolic changes that occur after spaying or neutering can cause some puppies to gain weight, often the real culprit for any weight gain is the human who feels guilty for subjecting their puppy to this medical procedure, and in an attempt to make themselves feel better, they feed more treats or meals to their companion.

If you notice weight gain after neutering or spaying your Lab puppy, simply adjust their food and treat consumption as needed and once stitches are healed, make sure that they are receiving adequate daily exercise.

Educate yourself with respect to vaccination

It has now become common practice to vaccinate adult dogs every three years, and if your veterinarian is insisting on a yearly vaccination for your puppy, you need to ask them why, because to do otherwise is considered by many professionals to be *"over vaccinating"*.

Whether or not your Lab actually needs a booster can be determined with a simple blood test at your vet's office, so be proactive, and ask for a blood test.

Puppies need to be vaccinated in order to provide them with protection against four common and serious diseases referred to as *"DAPP"*, which stands for Distemper, Adenovirus, Parainfluenza and Parvo Virus.

Approximately one week after your puppy has completed all three sets of primary DAPP vaccinations, they will be fully protected from those specific diseases.

Be aware of the Health Conditions that may affect your Happy Labrador

While a healthy Labrador may live to be 12 to 13 years or more, and with proper care may not suffer from any noted health problems, it's important to educate yourself and be aware of health concerns that have been known to affect this breed, such as some of the more common issues listed below:

Hip and Elbow Dysplasia: is a condition in which the head of the femur fits improperly into the hip or elbow joint socket. Factors that have an influence include nutrition, as this is a dog that suffers from obesity, a dog's environment and the condition of the hips of its parents. Screening for hip dysplasia is recommended for breeding stock.

Luxating Patella: this is a slipping kneecap condition that may also be caused by accidentally falling or jumping from a height. While surgery is the treatment option for this condition, many Labradors live a relatively normal life with this defect.

Exercise Induced Collapse (EIC): usually appears following short periods of strenuous exercise and can display as disorientation, weakness, collapse and hyperthermia, and dogs with this syndrome can live normal lives so long as they do not continue with intense training routines.

Megaesophagus: is an enlarged esophagus (the eating tube), and although not life-threatening, will require changes in your dog's eating habits, by feeding smaller portions more frequently with the dog in the sitting up position.

Mast Cell Tumors: are a form of cancer tumors originating from bone marrow and found within the connective tissues throughout the dog's body.

Melanoma: is more commonly found in the mouth of male dogs or on their toes. These tumors often travel deep into the bone of the dog's jaw or toes and quickly spread.

Hypothyroidism: is a condition resulting from an inadequate production of thyroid hormone, which is treated with medication. Symptoms can include weight gain or obesity, constant hunger, reduced energy and a coarser feel to the dog's coat texture. Blood samples will be taken in order to test for a malfunctioning thyroid.

Epilepsy: while the most common cause of seizures is an inherited form of epilepsy, they can be caused by many factors, including physical trauma, such as a head injury. If seizures begin, it will be very important to have your dog diagnosed and a medication treatment discussed.

Pyoderma: is a bacterial infection of the dog's skin that causes itching and redness that can lead to lesions on the skin that are similar to pimples. Treatment involves shampoo and antibiotic creams.

Seborrhea: is an incurable, inherited skin disorder causing either dry flaky skin (dandruff) or excessively oily skin, which can then cause inflammation and a secondary infection. This condition usually also causes the dog to be itchy and to smell bad as a result of the oil accumulation on the coat.

Your veterinarian will want to take blood tests and skin scrapings or a biopsy of the skin to test for parasites, as well as fungal and bacterial cultures to rule out allergies or digestive causes. Treatment will involve examination of your dog's diet and a combination of shampoos and conditioners to help relieve the condition.

Lick Granuloma: is a self-inflicted condition caused when the dog continually licks their lower legs or paws. This problem is considered to be a result of boredom, anxiety or stress resulting from an active and/or highly intelligent dog being left alone for long periods of time.

Diabetes: is one of the most common canine hormonal diseases that can occur at quite an early age (18-months) but may not be diagnosed until much later in the dog's life, between 7 and 10 years of age. Interestingly, 70% of diabetes is seen in female dogs.

Usually, the first sign of this disease is a normal appetite with an increased consumption of water and weight loss. Also, the sudden onset of cataracts may indicate an underlying diabetes cause and is a treatable condition requiring insulin injections to return the blood sugar levels to an acceptable level.

Obesity: many Labradors are overweight, simply because they love to eat and when love of eating is combined with little or no exercise, they will easily become obese. While obesity is a serious condition that plagues many breeds of dogs, the Labrador seems to be more prone to this health problem. The obvious treatment will be more exercise and/or less food.

Bloat (Emergency Gastrointestinal Syndrome): is a life-threatening, common occurrence that can affect any deep-chested canine. It can happen very quickly, especially if you feed your dog right after vigorous exercise, or if they are a very fast eater and gulp in large quantities of air with their food, which is often the case with the Labrador.

Bloat is a serious, life-threatening condition that requires immediate veterinary intervention. It is highly recommended that you get a slow feeder type of bowl to slow down this dog's often overly enthusiastic eating process and never feed them immediately after exercise or having had a large drink of water.

Educate yourself on Common Canine Diseases and Viruses

While your dog may never suffer from a common disease or virus, in order to ensure the safety and health of your happy Labrador, you need to be aware of the many common diseases and viruses that could detrimentally affect the health of your dog.

Always watch out for the symptoms of the following common diseases and if you suspect that your Lab has been infected, contact your vet immediately.

Distemper (sometimes called *"hard pad disease"*): is a contagious, serious, and deadly viral illness that is spread through the air or by direct or indirect contact with a dog (or other animal) that is already infected (such as ferrets, raccoons, foxes, skunks and wolves), that can also cause thickening of the pads on the feet or nose.

Early symptoms include fever, loss of appetite and mild eye inflammation that may only last a day or two, with symptoms becoming more serious and noticeable as the disease progresses. There is no known cure.

Adenovirus: causes infectious canine hepatitis, which can range in severity from very mild to very serious. The treatment focuses on management of symptoms, and the condition can sometimes result in death. Symptoms can vary and may include coughing, loss of appetite, increased thirst and urination, tiredness, vomiting and seizures.

Canine Parainfluenza Virus (CPIV): also referred to as *"canine influenza virus"*, *"greyhound disease"* or *"race flu"*, which is easily spread through the air or by coming into contact with respiratory secretions. While it is usually a self-limiting virus that will run its course within a couple of weeks, in severe cases and without antibiotic treatment, it may be fatal.

Symptoms can include a dry, hacking cough, difficulty breathing, wheezing, runny nose and eyes, sneezing, fever, loss of appetite, tiredness, depression and possible pneumonia. In cases where only a cough exists, tests will be required to determine whether the cause of the cough is the parainfluenza virus or the less serious *"kennel cough"*.

Canine Parvovirus (CPV): is a highly contagious viral illness affecting puppies and dogs, foxes, coyotes and wolves. Symptoms include vomiting, bloody diarrhoea, weight loss, and lack of appetite. Without prompt and proper treatment, dogs that have severe parvovirus infections can die within 48 to 72 hours.

Treatment will involve addressing dehydration and correcting electrolyte imbalances by administering intravenous fluids. Anti-inflammatory and antibiotic drugs are also given to control or prevent septicaemia, as well as drugs to control diarrhoea and vomiting.

Other Diseases and Viruses to Be Aware Of

What is Zoonotic? Zoonotic means a contagious disease that can be spread between both animals and humans.

Rabies: is a viral, zoonotic disease transmitted by coming into contact with the saliva of an infected animal, usually through a bite. The virus travels to the brain along the nerves and once symptoms develop (usually marked by a change in temperament), after a prolonged period of suffering, death is almost certainly inevitable. There is no treatment.

In most countries, vaccination against rabies is mandatory between the ages of twelve and sixteen weeks. If you plan to travel out of State or across country borders, you will need to make sure that your dog has an up-to-date Rabies Vaccination Certificate (NASPHV form 51) indicating they have been inoculated against rabies.

Leishmaniasis: is a contagious zoonotic infection caused by a parasite and is transmitted by a bite from a sand fly. While treatment involves the administration of a special drug (sodium stibogluconate), there is no definitive answer for effectively combating Leishmaniasis (especially since one vaccine will not prevent the known multiple species), with the prognosis often being fatal.

Symptoms include loss of appetite, diarrhoea, severe weight loss, exercise intolerance, vomiting, nosebleed, tarry feces, fever, pain in the joints, excessive thirst and urination, inflammation of the muscles, and death from kidney failure.

Lyme Disease: is one of the most common zoonotic tick-borne diseases in the world, which is transmitted by Borrelia bacteria found in the deer or sheep tick. Symptoms of this disease in a young or adult dog include recurrent lameness from joint inflammation, loss of appetite, depression, stiff walk with arched back, sensitivity to touch, swollen lymph nodes, fever, kidney damage, as well as rare heart or nervous system complications.

Control of the symptoms involves a lengthy course of antibiotic treatment in order to completely eliminate the organism.

Rocky Mountain Spotted Fever (RMSF): is a zoonotic disease transmitted by both the American dog tick and the RMSF tick, which must be attached to the dog for a minimum of five hours in order to transmit the disease.

Common symptoms include fever, reduced appetite, depression, painful joints, lameness, vomiting and diarrhoea, and some dogs may develop heart abnormalities, pneumonia, kidney failure, liver damage, or even neurological signs, such as seizures or unsteady, wobbly or stumbling gait. Treatment involves a 2-3 week course of antibiotics (Doxycycline or Tetracycline).

Ehrlichiosis: a tick-borne disease transmitted by both the brown dog tick and the Lone Star Tick, with common symptoms including depression, reduced appetite, fever, stiff and painful joints and bruising. The signs of infection typically occur less than a month after a tick bite and last for approximately four weeks. There is no vaccine available. Treatment involves a long course of antibiotics.

Anaplasmosis: deer ticks and Western blacklegged ticks are carriers of the bacteria that transmit canine Anaplasmosis. However, there is also another form of Anaplasmosis (caused by a different bacteria), that is carried by the brown dog tick.

Because the deer tick also carries other diseases, some animals may be at risk of developing more than one tick-borne diseases at the same time. Signs are similar to Ehrlichiosis and include painful joints, diarrhoea, fever, and vomiting, as well as possible nervous system disorders. Treatment involves administering the antibiotic Doxycycline for a 30-day period.

Tick Paralysis: this zoonotic infection is caused when ticks attach themselves to the skin and secrete a neurotoxin that affects the nervous system. Affected dogs show signs of weakness and limpness approximately one week after being first bitten.

Symptoms usually begin with a change in pitch of the dog's usual bark, and weakness in the rear legs that eventually involves all four legs, followed by the dog showing difficulty breathing and swallowing. Your dog can die if not diagnosed and properly treated by removal of the tick.

Canine Coronavirus: this highly contagious intestinal disease, which is spread through the feces of contaminated dogs, while now found worldwide, can be destroyed by most commonly available disinfectants. Symptoms include diarrhoea, vomiting and weight loss or anorexia. There is a vaccine available, which is usually given to puppies, because they are more susceptible at a young age. This vaccine is also given to show dogs that have a higher risk of exposure to the disease.

Leptospirosis: is a worldwide zoonotic bacterial infection that can affect humans and many different kinds of animals, including dogs. If left untreated, there is potential for both dogs and humans to die from this disease.

The good news is that this virus is usually treated with antibiotics and supportive care, and because you can protect your dog with a vaccination, it makes sense to vaccinate against this disease if you and your dog live in an area considered a hot spot for leptospirosis.

Be aware that allergies can adversely affect your dog's health

One of the most common complaints discussed at the veterinarian's office when they see dogs obsessively scratching, biting, licking and chewing at their skin or paws is possible allergies, and there can be many triggers. When you educate yourself, you can help ensure your Labrador never has to suffer from allergies and lead a healthier and happier life.

Environmental allergies: what many of us humans seem to forget is that our dogs can develop allergies to dust, chemicals, grass, mould, pollen, car exhaust, various forms of smoke, or flea and tick preparations, as well as allergies to materials such as wool or cotton, and chemicals found in washing soap or chemicals found in cleaning products you use around your home.

Visual symptoms are usually first noticed on the dog's stomach, inside of their legs, and at their tail or paws. Because many allergies are seasonal, our dogs will often be more affected in the spring or fall, with some airborne irritants inhaled by your dog resulting in coughing, sneezing or watery eyes.

Pay attention and if you think that your Lab may have come in contact with an irritant found somewhere in your environment, first give them a cleansing bath, with the proper canine shampoo and conditioner.

Junk food allergies: *"True"* food allergies usually account for only about 10% of allergy problems in our canine friends.

Be aware that itching, chewing and chronic ear infections are not actually caused by food allergies, but rather are the result of a suppressed immune system, which is the result of your dog eating a low-quality diet. Food sensitivity issues can often be completely resolved by changing your dog's diet to a high-quality food that is more easily digested.

For instance, check food ingredients because far too many dog food products contain gluten ingredients that are common allergens to our fur friends, such as corn, wheat and soybeans. Become a label reader and ask questions, before you choose your dog's food.

Take the time to learn a little canine CPR

Of course, nobody wants to find themselves in a situation where the life of their precious canine companion is put at risk. However, the reality is that accidents happen, and therefore knowing a little bit about how to help save your beloved furry friend is time well spent.

First of all, remember to handle an injured dog very carefully and gently. A dog that is traumatized, fearful or in pain, even one that is usually gentle, may lash out and try to bite.

Consider taking a class, because there are many animal CPR courses being offered these days through community educational systems or even online.

It's also a good idea to put together a canine first aid kit, both at home and in your vehicle, in case of emergencies, that includes the following items:

- Antiseptic Wash for wounds (hydrogen peroxide)
- Blanket
- Gauze Bandaging
- Kwik Stop styptic powder
- Medical Tape
- Nail Clippers
- Non-Stick Bandages for wounds
- Scissors
- Sterile Eye Wash
- Tick Twister
- Towel
- Tweezers
- Wash cloth

It would also be prudent to obtain a copy of the American Red Cross emergency techniques called *"Saving Your Pet With CPR"*, and familiarize yourself with the proper way to administer CPR to a dog.

Artificial Respiration Step by Step

If your Labrador becomes unconscious, depending upon what happened to them, they may stop breathing and if they stop breathing, they will go into cardiac arrest, when the heart stops beating and the dog dies.

However, after breathing stops, and before cardiac arrest, the heart can continue to beat for several minutes and this is when performing cardiopulmonary resuscitation (CPR) or artificial respiration can save your dog's life.

Step 1: place your dog on his or her side on a flat surface.

Step 2: check to make sure that your dog has actually stopped breathing by watching for the rise and fall of their chest and feel for their breath on your hand. Check the color of your dog's gums, because lack of oxygen will make them turn blue.

Step 3: check that the dog's airway is clear and there is nothing stuck in their mouth or throat by extending the head and neck and opening your dog's mouth.

If there is an object blocking their throat, pull the tongue outward and use your fingers or pliers to get a firm grip on the object so that you can pull it free from the dog's throat. If you cannot reach the object that appears to be blocking the dog's airway passage, you will have to use the Heimlich Maneuver to try and dislodge it (see below).

Step 4: so long as the dog's airway is not blocked, you can lift their chin to straighten out the neck and begin rescue breathing.

Step 5: hold the dog's muzzle and close their mouth, put your mouth over the dog's nose and blow gently – just enough to cause the dog's chest to rise.

Step 6: wait long enough for the air you just breathed into the dog's lungs to leave before giving another breath.

Step 7: continue giving one gentle breath every 3 seconds as long as the heart is still beating and until your dog starts to breathe on their own.

Canine Heimlich Manoeuvre

If breath won't go in, the airway may be blocked. In this case, you will need to turn your Lab upside down, with his or her back held against your chest.

Wrap your arms around the dog and clasp your hands together just below the dog's rib cage (since the dog is being held upside down, this will be actually above the rib cage, in the abdomen).

Using both arms, give five sharp thrusts to the abdomen, and then check the dog's mouth or airway for the object. If the object is visible, remove it, and give two more rescue breaths.

CPR Step by Step

If your Lab's heart has stopped beating, then CPR must be started immediately and ideal would be to have one person performing the artificial respiration, while the other performs the CPR.

Step 1: put your dog on his or her side on a flat surface.

Step 2: feel for your dog's pulse or heartbeat by placing one hand over his or her left side, just behind the front leg.

Step 3: place the palm of your hand on your dog's rib cage over his or her heart, with your other hand on top of the first (for puppies, put just your thumb on one side of the chest and the rest of your fingers on the other side).

Step 4: press down and release, compressing the dog's chest approximately one inch (2-3 centimetres) and squeeze and release 80 to 100 times every minute.

While it's always the hope that you may never need to, if your dog is not breathing and there is no pulse, knowing what steps to take in an emergency (which includes how to do the doggy Heimlich Manoeuvre or apply compressions), could literally save the life of your own dog or maybe even someone else's.

In a nutshell

While your dog may never suffer from any of the diseases known to occur in the Labrador breed, you will want to know what may afflict your dog because being aware of the signs can help them live a longer life. As well, familiarizing yourself with emergency CPR procedures in the following American Red Cross chart could help you save your dog's life.

It is also prudent to take the time to choose a veterinarian that can provide yearly check-ups, have your dog spayed or neutered in a timely fashion and educate yourself about required vaccinations.

Taking the steps outlined in this Chapter will help ensure that your adorable Lab will always stay healthy and happy in your lifelong journey.

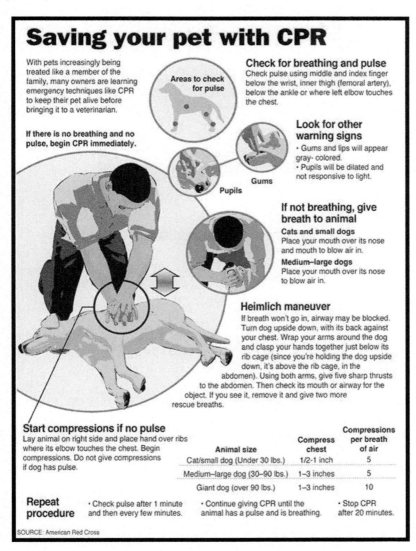

Saving your pet with CPR

With pets increasingly being treated like a member of the family, many owners are learning emergency techniques like CPR to keep their pet alive before bringing it to a veterinarian.

Areas to check for pulse

Check for breathing and pulse
Check pulse using middle and index finger below the wrist, inner thigh (femoral artery), below the ankle or where left elbow touches the chest.

If there is no breathing and no pulse, begin CPR immediately.

Look for other warning signs
• Gums and lips will appear gray- colored.
• Pupils will be dilated and not responsive to light.

Gums
Pupils

If not breathing, give breath to animal
Cats and small dogs
Place your mouth over its nose and mouth to blow air in.

Medium–large dogs
Place your mouth over its nose to blow air in.

Heimlich maneuver
If breath won't go in, airway may be blocked. Turn dog upside down, with its back against your chest. Wrap your arms around the dog and clasp your hands together just below its rib cage (since you're holding the dog upside down, it's above the rib cage, in the abdomen). Using both arms, give five sharp thrusts to the abdomen. Then check its mouth or airway for the object. If you see it, remove it and give two more rescue breaths.

Start compressions if no pulse
Lay animal on right side and place hand over ribs where its elbow touches the chest. Begin compressions. Do not give compressions if dog has pulse.

Animal size	Compress chest	Compressions per breath of air
Cat/small dog (Under 30 lbs.)	1/2-1 inch	5
Medium–large dog (30–90 lbs.)	1–3 inches	5
Giant dog (over 90 lbs.)	1–3 inches	10

Repeat procedure
• Check pulse after 1 minute and then every few minutes.
• Continue giving CPR until the animal has a pulse and is breathing.
• Stop CPR after 20 minutes.

SOURCE: American Red Cross

Chapter 4: Let Your Dog BE a Happy Dog

"Don't make the mistake of treating your dogs like humans, or they'll treat you like dogs."
— Martha Scott

This chapter is written to alert you to the fact that far too many of us humans have the tendency to treat our dogs more like human fur children than dogs.

You need to understand that not allowing your Labrador to be *"dog-like"* is very important when we're talking about THEIR happiness, because treating a dog like a human can ultimately result in <u>you</u> creating any number of behavioral issues.

<u>Your Lab is not a child</u>

While this might sound like a strange Chapter title, there is no doubt that many humans simply don't allow their dogs to actually BE dogs, because they are too busy confusing their dog by attributing human emotions to them, and treating them like children.

Yes, some dogs may need to wear cute clothing to keep warm and dry, however, many dogs (such as the Labrador), do not, and to make them wear coats, sweaters or funny hats is far more to appeal to the human that it ever will be because the dog likes it.

The Labrador is a working retriever with a strong sense of smell that was originally bred as a gun dog to hunt, track and retrieve in the water and in the field, which means that this dog loves to swim, get wet and dirty, play hard, run fast and retrieve.

Today's Labrador, when not being a working retriever, has a strong work ethic, and besides being an excellent participant in many canine sports, excels in many different working capacities, including bomb and drug detection, guide dog, therapy and disabled assistance work.

Every dog has a uniquely wonderful set of gifts to share with their human counterparts, if only us humans would listen. They *"tell"* us when they are unhappy, frightened, bored, nervous, and when they are under-exercised, yet often we do not pay attention, or we just think they are being badly behaved.

Many humans today are deciding to have dogs instead of children and then attempting to manipulate their dogs into being small (or large) furry children. This is having a seriously detrimental effect upon the health, happiness and behavior of our canine companions.

Single, lonely people often have dogs, which is just fine, so long as the human side of the equation doesn't expect their canine counterpart to fulfill what humans require on an emotional level, because this is very confusing to a dog who needs their human to lead them.

In order to be the best guardians for our dogs, we humans must have a better understanding of what our dogs need from us, rather than what we need from them, so that they can live in safety, harmony and security within our human environment.

Sadly, many of us humans are not well equipped to give our dogs what they really need and that is why there are so many homeless, abandoned and frustrated dogs and so many overflowing rescue facilities.

As a professional dog whisperer who is challenged with the task of finding amicable solutions for canine/human relationships that have gone off the rails, I can tell you with certainty that once humans understand what needs to be changed and actually take the steps to do the work required, almost every stressful canine/human relationship can be turned into a happy one.

The sad part is that many humans are simply not willing or able to really understand the breed they are choosing, or willing or able to do the consistent work and devote the time necessary to ensuring that their chosen dog's needs are met.

Almost ALL canine problems, both mentally and physically, are a direct result of ignorance or unwillingness on the part of the human guardian to choose the right dog and then learn what their dog truly needs.

First and foremost, our dogs need to be respected for their unique canine qualities.

For millennia, dog has been considered *"Man's best friend"*. In today's society, when we want to do the best for our canine companions and create a harmonious relationship, we humans need to spend more time receiving the proper training WE need, so that we can learn how us humans can be dog's best friend.

Any dog can be your *"best friend"* providing that YOU put in the work, and this is a universal truth that applies to any canine breed, including the Labrador.

If you are considering this enthusiastic and intelligent dog for your family, be certain that you can involve them in a wide variety of working tasks that will engage both their body and their mind, because doing so will ensure that you are raising a happy Labrador that never has to suffer from behavioral issues.

In a nutshell

It's important to understand that you actually need to let your dog BE a dog if you want to raise a happy and healthy companion. While treating them like a fur covered child may be something YOU need, it's not what THEY need, and can create much confusion that often will lead to behavioral issues later in life.

Chapter 5: Every Happy Labrador Wants Exercise

"No matter how little money
and how few possessions you own,
having a dog makes you rich."
— Louis Sabin

It cannot be stressed strongly enough how much this breed requires a vigorous daily exercise regimen for both a healthy body and mind.

If you cannot commit to the time required to ensure the Labrador receives plenty of engaging exercise each day, this will be a very unhappy dog that could develop multiple behavior issues.

Before we outline what this dog's daily minimum and ideal exercise requirements are, it may be helpful to first understand a little bit about what the Labrador was originally bred for and designed to do; this will give you some idea of what sorts of activities this dog will require when they are living as a companion within a human family.

Historical Origin of the Labrador

A native of Canada and then further developed in the United Kingdom, before they became your family companion, this sweet-faced, loveable dog was a highly prized hunting and waterfowl retrieving, purebred, gun dog.

The Labrador has a long history, originally known as the *"St. John's Water Dog"*, until they were renamed the *"Labrador Retriever"* when they were first imported from Canada to England.

Some historians of the breed believe that the Labrador may have originated in Portugal, before being introduced into Newfoundland by visiting Portuguese sailors.

The early beginnings of the Labrador can be traced as far back as late 1700's Newfoundland, when they were known as the "*Lesser and Greater St. John's dogs"*, and were used as working animals to haul carts full of fish, which is how they became known as a favorite fisherman's companion.

The Lesser Newfoundland had a smooth black coat and was well known to be a loyal and devoted companion, while the Greater St. John had a long thick coat. Both of these dog breeds became so well known for their excellent hunting and retrieving skills that news of their prowess reached Great Britain.

Apparently, the Earl of Malmesbury was so impressed with this dog's skill at retrieving anything in the water that after importing several dogs, he then devoted his entire kennel to stabilizing and further developing the Labrador breed.

Development of the modern Labrador Retriever is attributed to breeding practices of many dedicated Earls, Dukes and Lords who further developed this dog for duck hunting purposes on their estates during 19th century England, with the first Canadian dog believed to have arrived in England around 1820.

It was not until 1892 that the first liver or chocolate colored Labs were seen as a result of a breeding line created by the Duke of Buccleuch. Many historians believe that two dogs, named *"Avon and Ned"*, from the Duke of Buccleuch's breeding line are the ancestors of all modern Labradors.

The first yellow Labrador, the legendary *"Ben of Hyde"*, from which every yellow Lab is descended, was born in the year 1899 from two black-coated parents, and the Labrador was first imported to the United States during the First World War, after which this dog quickly became very popular.

The Labrador Retriever Club of Great Britain was instrumental in ensuring that the original purpose of this hunting breed was carefully preserved, and to this end, the Club requires all Labs to earn a Working Certificate for fieldwork, before they can be considered for any show competitions.

Recognized by the American Kennel Club (AKC) more than 100 years ago (in 1917) and by the United Kennel Club (UKC) in 1947, the high-spirited Labrador is an energetic hunting companion with a friendly and patient temperament.

It is evident from the historical origins information above that the Labradors were originally bred to assist hunters; they would run by their side and help them catch fallen wildfowl. Consequently, they were bred to be resilient, agile and muscular, which also means they naturally require lots of exercise (see below).

Minimum Daily Exercise Requirements

You will need to get your dog outside every day for a minimum of three, on leash, disciplined walks where they are walking at your side without pulling and paying close attention to your commands.

Once properly trained, the Labrador will also require at least a solid hour of freedom at a local dog park where they can run, play with other dogs or retrieve a ball or Frisbee, so get into the habit of a daily visit to your local dog park or a trip to the beach or forest.

This dog is a superior swimmer that loves water, so if you live near the ocean or a lake, take them to the beach and have them retrieve floats or sticks. If the water is cold, limit their time in the water so they don't suffer from hypothermia, because this dog will continue to retrieve if you continue to throw.

Ideal Daily Exercise Requirements

A fully-grown Labrador will need to burn off their daily pent-up energy by going for at least three good on-leash walks of 30 minutes to an hour every day. In order for this highly intelligent, energetic dog to be happy and well balanced, they ultimately need daily exercise far in excess of their regular walks.

This happy dog will need plenty of time to run freely beside a bike, jog beside a runner, run up the side of a mountain, swim to fetch sticks or floats or engage in a canine sport, such as Flyball or Agility, so they do not become bored, destructive, unhappy and overweight.

There is a long list of sports and services appropriate for the energetic and highly intelligent Labrador that includes, but is not limited to:

Obedience Competition – Agility – Dock Diving – Rally – Tracking – Hunting Trials – Field Trials – Canine Freestyle – Flyball – Canine Frisbee – Conformation Shows – Search and Rescue – Assistance Dogs for the Disabled – Guide Dogs for the Blind – Bomb Detection – Drug and Bug Detection – Medical Detection.

This dog likes to run, and a very good way to give them the amount of exercise they really need is to train them to jog beside your bicycle.

If you have access to a bicycle, consider training this dog to a *"Springer Bicycle Jogger",* so that they can receive a good amount of disciplined, vigorous exercise in a short period of time. You may find that you barely have to pedal and may wear out your breaks trying to slow down.

The *"Springer Bicycle Jogger"* attachment for a bicycle is an ideal and safe way to adequately exercise this intelligent and energetic dog while still keeping them under proper control, so that they cannot chase after a cat or other distraction.

The Springer easily attaches to any bicycle and the arm can be quickly removed when not needed. The large spring attaches to a harness on the dog and there is a quick release, break-away tab at the top of the rope in case the dog runs around one side of a pole while you and the bike are on the other side. As well, the large spring in this arrangement ensures that if your dog tries to lunge or chase a squirrel, you and your bicycle will remain stable.

Another form of fun exercise for a large and strong dog, like the Labrador, that is also fun for the humans, is the *"Dog Powered Scooter"*. This ingenious arrangement attaches the dog by harness to a scooter so that the dog becomes the power for the human riding the scooter (check them out online), and below is a picture from their website.

Ideal Living Conditions for a Happy Labrador

Without enough space, this large and enthusiastic working dog can often be like a bull in a china shop, accidentally knocking over everything, removing the contents of your coffee table with one swipe of their happily wagging tail or making that enticing peanut butter sandwich you just put in your 5-year-old's hand mysteriously disappear before you had time to blink twice.

Whenever the slightest hint of food is involved, you need to keep a vigilant and hyper watchful eye on this dog that will literally eat anything that is not securely guarded. The Labrador is one breed that will, if given the opportunity, literally eat himself to death, so be sure that all food remains securely out of reach.

You'll also find that it's very difficult to get mad at this dog that will do anything to please you, especially when they wag their tail so furiously and gaze lovingly at you with that sweet, innocent expression that could turn even the stoniest of hearts to mush.

The Labrador is a highly energetic companion who really needs to share a larger home space that ideally would include a large, securely fenced back yard or access to property where they can run and swim.

Do not think for a minute that a 4-foot fence will keep this dog in your back yard if they are bored or there's something more interesting going on beyond the perimeters.

Keep in mind that this dog can jump a fence much higher than you would ever imagine possible. I've actually witnessed a determined, considerably overweight, yet still highly athletic Lab named *"Stanley"* scale a 7-foot fence from a standing stop without thinking twice.

Please understand that this dog requires a substantial, daily disciplined and highly energetic exercise regimen that is designed to engage both their physical and mental faculties outside of the home. If you cannot commit to providing an active routine for the Labrador, this intelligent dog will very likely first become unhealthily overweight.

Next, an under-exercised Lab will lead to being bored and unhappy, which can then cause them to develop behavioral problems that could include acting out in destructive ways by chewing furniture (or other *"off limits"* items in the home), ingesting non-food items (which can lead to emergency surgery or death), digging holes in the garden, escaping the back yard and ultimately suffering from a prematurely shortened lifespan.

In order to raise a happy Labrador that will be a contented member of your family, it will be essential that you provide him or her with a large number of disciplined walks and plenty of rigorous daily exercise and/or canine sports in order to maintain a happy disposition and a healthy weight. This dog needs a LOT of exercise.

Never forget that dogs are pack animals, which means that it is not normal for them to be by themselves. When you adopt a dog into your family, you become their pack.

In other words, if you're planning to leave your Labrador alone for many hours every day, don't get a dog, because you will be contributing to your fur friend developing a depressed and unhappy state of mind.

As well, when a bored Lab has to find ways to entertain him or herself, you will also be opening the door to your dog developing unwanted behaviors, such as becoming destructive, barking for hours, raiding the garbage can, or attempting to escape so they can wander the neighborhood seeking activities that will exercise their body and stimulate their intelligent mind.

In a nutshell

The bottom line here is that the Labrador is a highly energetic canine, and learning a little bit about this dog's original history will help you to better understand how important plenty of daily exercise will be for helping keep him or her happy and healthy.

This Chapter also outlines many different canine sports and services that a Labrador may excel at, because involving your dog in a sport is a great way to provide them with the vigorous exercise they need, which will help to ensure that your dog is a healthy and happy family member.

Take away Tip: This dog needs a LOT of exercise.

Chapter 6: Feeding the Happy Labrador

"Dogs are not our whole life,
but they make our lives whole."
— Roger Caras

It's not rocket science to grasp the concept that a properly fed Labrador means a healthy, happy and longer-lived companion, so make sure that you spend the time to research high-quality food and treats for your happy Lab.

We are what we eat, and the same is absolutely true for our canine companions.

First, remember that our canine companions are carnivores, which means that they derive their energy and nutrient requirements and maintain their health by consuming a diet consisting mainly or exclusively of the flesh of animal tissues (in other words, meat).

When choosing an appropriate diet for your Labrador, considering the physiology of the canine's teeth, jaws and digestive tract will give you a better understanding of what food they should be eating.

Teeth, Jaws, and Digestive Tract

Teeth: canine teeth are all pointed because they are designed to rip, shred and tear into animal meat and bone.

Jaws: every canine is born equipped with powerful jaws and neck muscles for the specific purpose of being able to pull down and tear apart their hunted prey.

The jaw of every canine opens widely to hold large pieces of meat and bone, while the actual mechanics of the canine jaw permits only vertical (up and down) movement that is designed for crushing.

Digestive Tract: the canine digestive tract is short, simple and designed to move their natural choice of food (hide, meat and bone) quickly through their systems.

We humans need vegetables and plant matter in our diet and have the flat molars to effectively crush and chew them. While we often believe our dogs require the same, when choosing an appropriate food source for your Lab, you need to consider that vegetables and plant matter require more time to break down in the gastrointestinal tract. This in turn, requires a more complex digestive system, that the canine body simply does not have.

The canine digestive system is simply unable to break down vegetable matter, which is why whole vegetables look pretty much the same going into your dog, as they do coming out the other end.

Consider how much healthier and long-lived your beloved Labrador can be if, instead of largely ignoring nature's design for our canine companions, we chose to feed them whole, unprocessed, species-appropriate food.

Whatever you decide to feed your dog, keep in mind that, just as too much wheat or other grains and fillers in our human diet are having detrimental effects on our health, the same can be very true for our dogs.

Read the labels so that you can be certain to avoid foods that contain fillers or high amounts of grains, that are inappropriate for a healthy canine diet.

Control of Your Happy Labrador's Food

The Labrador has a reputation for being always hungry and their strong sense of smell will alert this dog to any potential food source, edible or otherwise. Conscientious guardians will need to carefully oversee the feed bowl and exactly what this dog puts in its mouth to ensure that he or she does not become overweight.

You will also need to make certain that you don't leave any food out on the countertop and you don't provide a way that your dog can easily access the garbage can; if you do, it's almost guaranteed that a Labrador left alone will lick the counters clean and eat anything remotely hinting of food they may find in the garbage can. I knew a dog once that ate an entire pound of butter that was left out on the counter, causing a very sick puppy.

It's important that your Lab understands that YOU are in control of their food source. Once they understand this, they will also figure that there will be windows of opportunity for receiving and eating their food, and this routine will help to develop healthy eating habits.

Many people use a scoop or measuring cup to put dry food into their dog's bowl. This is a mistake, because it's very important to mix your dog's food with your hands, so that your scent is all over the food, before you give it to them to eat. This sends a "message" to your Lab that you are their pack leader, because it mimics what would happen if you were the alpha dog out hunting for your food in the wild.

For instance, while a pack of wild dogs hunting for food all work hard to capture their prey, the alpha pack leader always gets to eat first while all the other dogs must wait until the leader of the pack eats their fill, before they can rush in to eat what is left over.

Therefore, when you are mixing your domesticated dog's dinner with your hands, you are sending them the subtle message that you are the pack leader, you've already eaten your fill and you are now allowing them to eat what was left over.

Feeding Puppies

A general rule of thumb for growing Lab puppies is to feed daily amounts of between 2 and 3% of what the puppy's adult weight is projected to be or 10% of the puppy's current body weight. You will want to keep in mind that while all puppies require extra protein during the first two years of their life to help them develop into healthy adult dogs, this is especially important with higher energy puppies.

There are now many foods on the market that are formulated for all stages of a dog's life (including the puppy stage). Whether you choose one of these foods or a food specially formulated for puppies, they will need to be fed smaller meals more frequently throughout the day (3 or 4 times), until they are at least one year of age.

Feeding Adults

Choose foods that list high-quality meat protein as the main ingredient and, depending on your dog's particular energy level, feed between 2 and 3% of their body weight every day. While some dogs prefer one meal a day, most will appreciate morning food (after a walk) and evening food (after a walk).

Be careful not to get caught up in "convenience" when you are out grocery shopping for yourself, and decide to buy your Lab's food at the same place, because most grocery stores do not carry the best dog food.

Instead, make the time to visit your local pet store, talk with educated representatives, avoid grains, and choose quality sources of meat protein for healthy puppies and dogs, including beef, buffalo, chicken, duck, fish, hare, lamb, ostrich, pork, rabbit, turkey, venison, or any other source of wild meaty protein.

Treats

There are endless choices of dog treats lining the shelves of every feed store, pet store, and grocery store, and it will be an overwhelming task to choose wisely, unless you keep one simple rule in mind, and choose treats that contain only one ingredient or very few ingredients.

Whatever reason you choose to give treats to your Labrador, keep in mind that if we treat our dogs too often throughout the day, they can become overweight, and we may create a picky eater who will no longer want to eat their regular meals.

As well, researchers in Sweden have discovered that dogs were happier when they had to earn their treats as a reward for completing a task, rather than just being given a treat for looking cute, because just like us humans who get that happy "eureka" moment when we finally solve a problem, the same is true for our canine counterparts.

Dangerous Treats

Always carefully read labels and take note of where treats are manufactured, because not all countries have the most stringent manufacturing protocols, and honestly there are many treats that you absolutely should NOT be feeding your dog, including:

Rawhide, which is soaked in an ash/lye solution to remove every particle of meat, fat and hair and then further soaked in bleach to remove remaining traces of the ash/lye solution. Now that the product is no longer food, it no longer has to comply with food regulations.

The wet rawhide is shaped into chews, and once dry it shrinks to approximately 25% of its original size before arsenic-based products are used as preservatives, and antibiotics and insecticides are added to kill bacteria.

While rawhide chews are tough and long lasting, when a dog chews a rawhide treat, they ingest many harsh chemicals. Also, when your dog swallows a piece of rawhide, that piece can swell up to four times its size inside your dog's stomach, which can cause anything from mild to severe gastric blockages that could become life threatening and require surgery.

Pig's Ears are very attractive to most dogs that will eagerly devour them. However, they are thin, crispy and very high in fat, which can cause stomach upsets, vomiting and diarrhoea. In addition, pieces can break off and become stuck in a dog's throat.

Also, pig ears are often processed and preserved with unhealthy chemicals that discerning dog guardians will not want to feed their dogs.

Hoof Treats are actual cow, horse and pig hooves that humans believe are healthy, *"natural"* treat choices for their dogs when the truth is that after processing with harsh chemicals, preservatives and antibiotics, they retain little, if any, of their *"natural"* qualities.

Also, hooves are very hard and can cause the chipping or breaking of your dog's teeth as well as perforation or blockages in your dog's intestines.

Healthy Treats

There are so many healthy treat choices available, which means that there is no excuse for feeding your Lab unhealthy, nutrient-deficient treats. Read the labels to make sure the treats you are choosing are appropriately sized for your dog and are of the highest quality. Examples of healthy treats include:

Hard Treats: come in many varieties of shapes, sizes and flavors and will help to keep your dog's teeth cleaner.

Soft Treats: are also available in endless varieties and flavors, suitable for all the different needs of our furry friends and are often smaller in size and used for training purposes.

Dental Treats or Chews: are designed with the specific purpose of helping your dog to maintain healthy teeth and gums by exercising the jaw and massaging gums, while removing plaque build-up near the gum line.

Freeze-Dried and Jerky Treats: offer a tasty morsel most dogs find irresistible as they are usually made of simple, meaty ingredients, such as liver, poultry and seafood. Be careful when choosing jerky treats, as they are often processed with too much salt.

Human Food Treats: be very careful when feeding human foods to dogs as treats, because many of our foods contain unhealthy additives, such as salt, sugar and other ingredients that could be toxic and harmful.

Also educate yourself about the common human foods that are actually poisonous to our canine friends, such as grapes, raisins, onions and chocolate, to name a few.

Generally, the treats you feed your Lab should not make up more than approximately 10% of their daily food intake, so make sure the treats you choose are high quality, with single or few ingredients so that you can help to keep your dog both happy and healthy.

The Right Food for Your Happy Labrador

"Dog Food" has significantly changed since1785, when the English Sportman's Dictionary described the best diet for a dog's health in an article entitled *"Dog"*. This article indicated that the best food for a dog was something called *"Greaves"*, described as "the sediment of melted tallow made into cakes for dogs' food".

From these meager beginnings, commercially-made dog food has become a massively lucrative industry that has only fairly recently evolved beyond feeding our dogs the dregs of human leftovers, because it was cheap and convenient for us.

Even today, the majority of dog food choices often have far more to do with being convenient for humans to store and serve, than it does with being a diet truly designed to be a nutritionally balanced, healthy food choice for our canine companions.

Educating yourself by talking to experts and reading everything you can find on the subject, plus taking into consideration several relevant factors, will help to answer the dog food question for you and your dog.

For instance, where you live may dictate what sorts of foods you have access to, while other factors to consider will include the particular requirements of your dog, such as their age, energy and activity levels.

Our dogs are also suffering from many of the same life-threatening diseases that are commonly found in our human society (heart disease, cancer, diabetes, obesity), which all have a direct correlation with over-feeding and/or eating genetically altered foods that are no longer pure, in favor of a convenient, processed and packaged diet.

Different Types of Food Choices

The Raw Diet: raw feeding advocates believe that the ideal diet for their dog is one which would be very similar to what a dog living in the wild would have access to while hunting or foraging.

These canine guardians are often opposed to feeding their dog any sort of commercially manufactured pet foods, because they consider them to be poor substitutes, and for the most part, I would agree.

Many guardians of high energy, working breed dogs will agree that their dogs thrive on a raw or BARF (Biologically Appropriate Raw Food) diet and strongly believe that the potential benefits of feeding a raw dog food diet are many, including:

- Healthy, shiny coats
- Decreased shedding
- Fewer allergy problems
- Healthier skin
- Cleaner teeth
- Fresher breath
- Increased energy levels
- Improved digestion
- Smaller stools
- Strengthened immune system
- Increased mobility in arthritic pets
- Increase or improvement in overall health

A raw diet is a direct evolution of what dogs ate before they became our domesticated pets and we turned toward commercially prepared, easy-to-serve dry dog food that required no special storage or preparation.

The Dehydrated Diet: is available in both raw and cooked meat forms, which are usually air dried to reduce moisture and inhibit bacterial growth. While the appearance of dehydrated dog food is very similar to dry kibble, the typical feeding methods include adding warm water before serving, which makes this type of diet both healthy for our dogs and convenient for us to serve.

Dehydrated recipes are made from minimally processed fresh, whole foods to create a healthy and nutritionally balanced meal that retains more of the overall nutritional value, and will meet or exceed the dietary requirements of a healthy canine.

A dehydrated diet is a convenient way to feed your dog a nutritious diet, because all you have to do is add warm water and wait five minutes while the food re-hydrates so your dog can enjoy a warm meal.

The Kibble Diet: there is no mistaking that the convenience and relative economy of dry dog food kibble, which had its beginnings in the 1940's, continues to be the most popular pet food choice for many dog-friendly humans. Thankfully, there are now many high-quality kibble foods available.

The Right Bowl for the Labrador: there are many different types and categories of dog bowls, including Automatic Watering, Elevated, Ceramic, Stoneware, No Skid, No Tip, Slow Feeder, Stainless, Wooden and Travel Bowls.

Keeping in mind that the Labrador is highly food motivated and that they can suffer from dangerous bloat, you will definitely want to get this voracious eater a **slow feeder** type of bowl to slow down the speed at which they consume their food.

In a nutshell

While food and treat choices for your favorite furry Labrador can be overwhelming, a basic understanding of canine physiology and making wise decisions concerning all the many different types of food available, will help you to add many healthy and happy years to your dog's life.

When you choose a brand and type of food for your adorable Labrador, you are the sole protector of your furry companion and I cannot stress strongly enough the important of a well thought out choice. This can not only elongate the length of your dog's life by avoiding conditions, such as high blood pressure or bladder stones, but also make your dog have optimal health and feel good and happy!

Chapter 7: Care of the Happy Labrador

"Dogs' lives are too short.
Their only fault, really."
— Agnes Sligh Turnbull

Imagine you are travelling by car on a daily basis without being protected by a seatbelt or an airbag. How safe would you feel? Unfortunately, this is the reality for lots of our furry friends, because their guardians have neglected their safety responsibilities.

Now, imagine going for months without washing your hair, cutting your nails or brushing your teeth. Again, that is the reality for many dogs, because their owners have not been advised on the importance of good grooming. How happy and well-behaved do you think such an ill-cared for dog would be?

The following few paragraphs outline safe travelling, licensing, insurance and grooming requirements, all of which can help to ensure that your Labrador is safe, legal and better cared for at the vet's office.

Keep in mind that if your Lab is safely secured when travelling, they might not be dead or seriously injured should you be involved in a vehicle accident. We humans wear seatbelts to be safe – what about safety for our best fur friends?

Further, if your dog is properly licensed, they will be returned to you should they go missing, and this is a much happier dog than one spending who knows how long behind bars at a rescue or SPCA.

As well, if you have pet health insurance, chances are that they will be better cared for at the vet's office, which means a healthier and happier dog.

Tips for Keeping Your Dog Safe

Not So Safe Harness Restraints: is your canine companion safe when buckled into a safety harness for travel in vehicles? Be aware that many of the dog harnesses in the marketplace have a 100% failure rate.

If you cannot find a safety harness that is actually been strength tested and crash tested (i.e. optimal choice), the safest travel arrangement for any dog is to secure them inside a kennel, that is bolted to the floor or secured with the vehicles seatbelt.

Kennels: a dog kennel or crate will easily fit (sideways) on the back seat of most vehicles and can be secured with the vehicle's restraint system. A Lab riding inside a kennel that is secure inside your vehicle will have the best protection in the case of a rollover accident, plus you will avoid the fines some locations are now levying for allowing a dog to roam freely inside a moving vehicle.

Air Travel: while the Labrador puppy (depending on age) may be small enough to fit into a soft Sherpa bag for travel inside an airplane cabin (as carry-on baggage), they will be much too large to travel inside the airplane cabin when they are fully grown, and will need to be transported inside a heated cargo hold.

Licensing: when you purchase your Lab a yearly license or identifying tag, they will be legal, and should they become lost when wearing a license, there is a much higher possibility that your dog will be returned to you, instead of spending their last few days behind bars at the local SPCA or rescue facility.

Pet Health Insurance: purchasing health insurance for your dog means that they will usually live a longer, healthier and happier life, because they will receive better care throughout their life.

Be aware that you need to start insurance when your Lab is a young puppy, because waiting until they are older will mean that your monthly premiums are considerably higher.

Grooming Your Dog

Regular grooming is important for a happy and healthy Labrador, because it keeps them clean, their skin moisturized and bug free, plus grooming time can alert you to any problems before they become more serious.

Unless you are paying someone else to professionally groom your dog, there will be a basic arsenal of equipment and products you will need to purchase so that you can keep your happy Labrador looking his or her best.

Also, you will want to get your dog used to their grooming routine early on, because otherwise, every time your dog needs to be groomed will end up being a traumatic experience for both dog and human that can last for many years.

For instance, I've been asked to groom dogs that have been kicked out of every grooming salon because their owners did not take the time to introduce the puppy to bath time, nail clipping and other necessary grooming procedures at a young age.

I can tell you from much personal experience that having to groom a writhing, screaming dog that is all teeth, because they are fighting the procedure, is hell on wheels. Try going through this with an unwilling, 80-pound (36.2 kg) Labrador and you will very soon be wishing your companion were a goldfish.

Grooming Equipment You Will Need

A standard arsenal of equipment that will help you keep your Labrador looking their best will include a brush to remove dead hair and help distribute natural oils, a rake to help remove shedding undercoat during molting, a pair of nail clippers, and a flea comb and tick twister (just in case).

A bristle brush – is the ideal tool for removing debris and dead hair from the Labrador coat, while at the same time distributing natural oils to keep the coat looking healthy and shiny.

A rake – is very helpful for removing dead hair when your puppy is changing from their puppy coat to the new adult coat or during twice-yearly molting, when the dog may blow their undercoat.

Nail clippers or scissors (and/or a slow speed pet Dremel™) – will be tools you need to use every couple of weeks or more, depending on how quickly your Lab's nails grow and what types of surfaces they may be walking on.

Flea comb – hopefully you won't ever need one, however, as the name suggests, these combs are designed for the specific purpose of removing fleas from a dog's coat. Usually small in size for maneuvering in tight spaces, they may be made of plastic or metal with the teeth of the comb placed very close together to trap hiding fleas.

Tick Twister – hopefully your dog won't ever get a tick, but if they do, this is a simple device for painlessly, easily and quickly removing ticks that have imbedded themselves in your dog's skin.

Grooming Products You Will Need

Products you will need to invest in when grooming your Labrador yourself will include shampoos, conditioners, creams, lotions, sprays and powders.

Shampoos: NEVER make the mistake of using human shampoo or conditioner, that has a pH balance of 5.5, for bathing your Labrador; our canine companions have an almost neutral pH balance of 7.5, and any shampoo with a lower pH will be harmful to your dog, because it will strip the natural oils and be too harshly acidic for their coat and skin. This in turn can create skin problems and allow for a very unhappy dog.

Conditioners: taking the extra time to condition your Lab's coat will not only make it look and feel better, it will also add additional benefits, including:

- Preventing the escape of natural oils and moisture
- Keeping the coat cleaner for a longer period of time
- Repairing a coat that has become dull, damaged or dry
- Restoring a soft, silky feel
- Helping the coat dry more quickly
- Protecting from the heat of the dryer and breakage of hair

The benefits of spending the extra two minutes to condition your dog's coat will be appreciated by both yourself and your dog that will have overall healthy skin and a coat with a natural shine.

Oops, My Dog Has Fleas

You haven't been paying attention and now realize that your dog is suffering from an infestation of fleas. Now is the time to bathe them with shampoo containing pyrethrum (a botanical extract found in small, white daisies) or a shampoo containing citrus or tea tree oil.

Also, you can bathe and spray them with the non-toxic and highly effective CedarCide products, which can also be used to spray down their bedding and any carpets in the home, and will kill fleas on contact without harming anyone.

CedarCide is a company that makes 100% safe, organic products to control biting bugs on your furry friends without worrying about harmful chemicals that are not good for you, your children or your canine companions.

Simply spray it on and bugs of any sort that come into contact with the solution will be dead, while your dog's coat will be shiny and fresh smelling, like the inside of a cedar chest.

Nail Care

Many canine guardians neglect taking proper care of their Lab's toenails, which can lead to many problems later in life, such as painful joints and difficulty walking, which will make for a very unhappy dog.

Purchase a good pair of clippers and learn how to do this every two to three weeks.

Styptic Powder: you will always want to avoid causing any pain when trimming your Labrador's toenails, because you don't want to destroy their trust in you regularly performing this necessary task.

However, accidents do happen, therefore if you accidentally cut into the vein in the toenail, know that you will cause your dog pain, and that the toenail will bleed. Therefore, it is always a good idea to keep some styptic powder (often called *"Kwik Stop")* in your grooming kit.

Dip a moistened finger into the powder and apply it with pressure to the end of the bleeding nail, because this is the quickest way to stop a nail from bleeding in just a few seconds.

Some dogs prefer having their nails trimmed with a rotary "Dremel" type of device that grinds down the excess nail and it is easier to avoid cutting into the vein. Keep in mind that if you decide to trim your dog's nails this way, you will have to purchase a "doggy Dremel" made especially for this purpose, because using your shop Dremel will harm your dog's nails as it is too high speed and will burn the nails.

Ear Care

Dogs can often suffer from painful ear infections, especially those with long, pendant ears (like the Labrador) that like to swim, because these ears can easily trap moisture.

Paying attention and keeping your Lab's ears clean and dry will prevent this type of unhappy pain and suffering. Make sure that you keep ear powders and cleaning solutions in your grooming kit, because with proper preventative care, your dog need never suffer from an ear infection.

Ear Powders: which can be purchased at any pet store, are designed to help keep your dog's ears dry while at the same time inhibiting the growth of bacteria that can lead to infections. Ear powders are also used when removing excess hair growth from inside a dog's ear canal, as the powder makes it easier to grip the hair.

Ear Cleaning Solutions: your local pet store will offer a wide variety of ear cleaning creams, drops, oils, rinses or wipes specially formulated for cleaning your Lab's ears.

In addition, there are many home remedies that will just as efficiently clean your dog's ears without the high price tag, including Witch Hazel (a 50:50 solution of Organic Apple Cider Vinegar and Purified Water) or a 50:50 solution of Hydrogen Peroxide and Purified Water.

Teeth Care

Another greatly overlooked area in your happy Labrador's health is ensuring that their teeth are clean and properly looked after, so that they don't suffer from loose or broken teeth, and plaque build-up that leads to painful gum disease. You know how miserable a toothache can be – imagine your poor dog who cannot tell you how unhappy they are.

Many guardians use the excuse that *"my dog doesn't like it"* when they try to brush their dog's teeth, and overlook the fact that in order to keep their entire dog healthy, they <u>must</u> have healthy teeth and the only way to ensure this, is to brush their dog's teeth every day.

Canine Toothpastes: are flavoured with beef or chicken in an attempt to appeal to the dog's taste buds, while some contain baking soda, which is the same mild abrasive found in many human pastes, and are designed to gently scrub the teeth.

Other types of canine toothpastes are formulated with enzymes that are designed to work chemically by breaking down tartar or plaque in the dog's mouth. While these pastes don't need to be washed off your dog's teeth and are safe for them to swallow, whether or not they remain on the dog's teeth long enough to do any good might be debatable.

Just as effective for killing germs, whitening and cleaning your dog's teeth, and much less expensive than fancy pastes, is old-fashioned hydrogen peroxide; you can combine hydrogen peroxide (3% food grade), aloe vera juice (1:1) with a little bit of baking soda.

Paw Care

If your dog runs over sharp barnacles on the beach, jogs with you on hard road surfaces, or over other rough surfaces this can cause cuts and scrapes and very rough surfaces on the paws. If you live in a hot climate, be aware that sidewalks, road surfaces and sandy beaches can get extremely hot for your Lab's feet.

Paw Creams: depending upon activity levels and the types of surfaces our canine counterparts usually walk on, they may suffer from cracked or rough pads. You can restore resiliency and keep your Labrador's paws in healthy condition by regularly applying a cream or lotion to protect their paw pads. A good time to do this is just after you've clipped their nails.

In a nutshell

Learning about simple steps that will keep your Labrador safe, and what's involved in keeping him or her properly groomed will go a long way toward helping them to live a long, happy and healthy life.

While for many people the concept of grooming your dog conjures up notions of brushes and bows, it is in fact a vital element to their overall health and wellbeing. Regularly grooming your Labrador will help you detect any underlying diseases or conditions early and will allow your beloved fur friend to feel better and live longer and happier.

Chapter 8: Are YOU the Ideal Happy Labrador Guardian?

"You think those dogs will not be in heaven!
I tell you they will be there long before any of us."
— Robert Louis Stevenson

If you have not chosen wisely when sharing your life with a canine companion, you are setting yourself, your family, your friends and your neighbours up for many years of stress and unhappiness.

It is vitally important that you take a good hard look at your own energy level and lifestyle, ask yourself some serious questions that you honestly answer, and not scrimp on taking the time to do plenty of research about the breed of dog you may be considering.

Sharing your life with a canine friend should never be undertaken lightly, or on a whim or spur of the moment decision, or because you like the colour of a dog's coat.

Before you can learn how to become your dog's ideal guardian, you need to first have no doubt in your mind that you have the energy, commitment, time and skill level necessary to raise a happy dog. Once

The Happy Labrador

this is established in the affirmative, you then need to know how to choose the right breed of puppy or dog.

Choosing the <u>right</u> puppy for your family and your lifestyle is more important than you might imagine, and far too many people forget to consider how important is to choose a puppy or dog based on compatibility with their own energy and lifestyle.

For instance, many humans choose a puppy (or older dog) for all the wrong reasons, including because:

- they like what it looks like
- the breed may currently be popular
- the breed appeared on TV or in a movie they enjoyed
- their parents had the same kind of dog when they were a child
- a friend has the same breed
- they feel sorry for a homeless dog
- a friend or family member can no longer keep their dog
- the children are begging for a dog

While some of these above reasons can be honourable, the most important reasons for choosing to share your life with a particular canine companion has not been properly considered.

In order to make an intelligent choice that will bring happiness to everyone, you need to take a serious look at your life as it is today and also how you envision it to be during the next ten to fifteen years, and then ask yourself several very important questions, including:

Activity – Do I lead a highly active, medium or low-intensity life? For instance, am I out jogging the streets every morning, hiking local mountains or riding my bicycle five miles to the local grocery store, or does my job or leisure time activity keep me in front of the computer or on the couch watching movies?

Travel – Do I travel a lot for work or pleasure? If you don't, choose a small dog that can travel with you in the plane cabin; your loyal dog will be unhappy without you or you will have greatly increased expenses, because you will have to hire a dog sitter or leave them in a kennel.

Allergies – Do I prefer a very tidy house? Do I have allergies? Many breeds shed their hair all year round and your entire house and everything you own will be covered with dog hair. This means more frequent housework and if you or your family members have allergies, as much as they may enjoy the company of a furry friend, if you decide to proceed, better would be to choose a non-shedding breed.

Time – Does my family take up all my spare time and are my children old enough to handle a puppy? A dog is like a child that never grows up and in order for them to be happy and well-behaved family members, they require a lot of your daily time and attention.

Fitness – Am I physically fit and healthy enough to be out there walking a dog two to three times a day, every day, rain or shine, and much more during the puppy stage?. If I've chosen a highly active breed, do I have the time to involve them in a canine sport?

Cost – Am I able to afford the extra food costs and the veterinarian expenses that are part of being a conscientious dog guardian?

Commitment – Is the decision to bring a puppy or dog into my life a family decision, or just because the children, who may quickly lose interest, have been begging for a dog?

Why? – What is the number one reason why I want a dog in my life?

Once you ask yourself these important questions and honestly answer them, you will have a much better understanding of whether you have what it takes to share your life with a dog, and perhaps the beginning insight of the type of puppy or dog that would be best suited for you and your family.

If you are too busy for a dog, or choose the wrong dog that is not compatible with you or your family's energy and lifestyle (or don't really have the time and commitment necessary to properly socialize and raise a canine companion), you will inevitably end up with an unhappy dog, which will lead to behavioral issues, which then will lead to a stressed family, angry neighbors, and extra expenses to hire a professional to help you reverse unwanted behavioral problems.

Even worse, an incompatible choice can mean that you may end up contributing to the already overflowing crisis of another dog being abandoned at the local SPCA or kill shelter.

Once you have absolutely determined that the Labrador is the right dog for you (see next Section: The Ideal Guardian), rather than simply leaving it to chance, you need to choose the right puppy from the litter.

Generally speaking, when choosing a puppy out of a litter, look for one that is friendly and outgoing, rather than one who is overly aggressive or fearful.

Visit the breeder and take note of a puppy's social skills when they are still with their littermates, because this will help you to choose the right puppy for your family. Puppies who demonstrate good social skills with their littermates are much more likely to develop into easy-going, happy adults who play well with other dogs.

In a social setting where all the puppies can be observed together, there are several important observations you can make, including:

Play – Notice which puppies are comfortable both on top and on the bottom when play fighting and wresting with their littermates, and which puppies seem to only like being on top. Puppies who don't mind being on the bottom or who appear to be fine with either position will usually play well with other dogs when they become adults.

Sharing – Observe which puppies try to keep the toys away from the other puppies and which puppies share. Those who want to hoard the toys and keep all other puppies away may be more aggressive with other dogs over food or treats, or in play where toys are involved as they become older.

Company – Notice which puppies seem to like the company of the other pups and which ones seem to be loners. Puppies who like the company of their littermates are more likely to be interested in the company of other dogs as they mature than anti-social puppies.

Compassion – Observe the reaction of puppies that get yelped at when they bite or roughhouse with another puppy too hard. Puppies who ease up when another puppy yelps or cries are more likely to respond appropriately when they play too roughly as adults.

Sociability – Check to see if the puppy you are interested in is sociable with people, because if they will not come to you, or display fear of strangers, this may develop into a fear/aggression problem when they become adults.

Handling – Check if the puppy you are interested in is relaxed about being handled, because if they are not, they may become difficult or overly nervous around adults and children during daily interactions, during grooming or while visiting the veterinarian's office.

Is Your Happy Puppy Healthy?

While mental health is very important, you will also want to do all you can to determine if your chosen puppy is physically healthy.

First, ask to see veterinarian reports from the breeder to satisfy yourself that the puppy is as healthy as possible, and then once you make your decision to share your life with a particular puppy, and they are old enough to bring home, make an appointment with your own veterinarian for a complete examination.

However, before you take your new puppy home, there are general signs of good health to be aware of, including the following:

Body Fat – a healthy puppy will look round and well fed, with an obvious layer of fat over their rib cage.

Breathing – a healthy puppy will breathe quietly, without coughing, wheezing or sneezing.

Coat Condition – a healthy puppy will not be itchy and will have a soft coat with no dandruff, dullness, greasiness or bald spots.

Energy Level – a well-rested puppy will be alert and energetic.

Hearing – a healthy puppy should react if you clap your hands or snap your fingers behind their head.

Genitals – a healthy puppy will not have any sort of discharge visible in or around their genital or anal regions.

Mobility – a healthy puppy will walk and run normally without wobbling, limping or seeming to be weak, stiff or sore.

Vision – a healthy puppy will have bright, clear eyes without crust or discharge and they should notice if a ball is rolled past or a toy is tossed within their field of vision.

The Ideal Guardian

Once you have established that you have what it takes to share your life with a dog (by considering the questions in the previous Section), you should consider the following tips to determine whether the Labrador would be the right breed for you and your family.

The Labrador will be an excellent choice for highly active individuals or families with all ages of children as they are friendly, patient and playful. This dog can also be a good companion for older adults who have the energy, time and mobility required to provide this dog with the daily exercise and mental stimulation they need.

Keep in mind that while the Labrador will usually be social and accepting of both unknown dogs and humans, when not trained to live a calm life, they can suffer from attachment issues if expected to spend many hours alone.

The ideal guardian for a the Happy Labrador will be a highly energetic, outdoor loving person (or family) that is aware of this dog's tendency to overeat, enjoys hunting, swimming, biking, jogging, working outdoors, is able to spend a high percentage of their day outside, or who has the time to enroll this dog in any manner of energetic canine sports.

As an example, the ideal happy Labrador guardian will be an early riser, that gets into their jogging or biking gear and is out on the street or running a 10-mile forest trail even before breakfast.

After returning home, everyone will have their breakfast and then (since you work at home) your dog can rest for a couple of hours while you work on your computer before it's time to leash up your companion and head off to the local dog park for a game of Frisbee or play with other dogs.

Back home for a midday snack for your dog and lunch for you, while you take time (depending on this dog's age) to teach basic commands, or maybe some tricks before your dog has a snooze and you get back to your computer.

Now it's about 4:00 pm and again it's time to get you and your dog outside for some serious exercise that may involve hooking your Labrador onto a Springer bicycle jogger or taking you for a roll as the power for your Dog Powered Scooter for 30 to 40 minutes. Don't forget to give them a chance to empty their bowels and drain their bladder.

Back home and time to prepare dinner for both dog and human, then after dinner (again depending on the age of your dog) perhaps a few more minutes of basic command and/or trick training before you each have some lazy time in front of the fire or TV screen.

Now it's getting to be later evening and before bed you need to put your Labrador on leash and take them outside for a quick walk around the block, so they can drain out their bladder before bed.

Everyone now in his or her respective beds as both human and dog have a rejuvenating sleep before the start of the next day when you do this all over again.

Of course, this is just one scenario that would be excellent for the Happy Labrador, and with a little imagination on your part, there are many others that would fit the bill quite nicely.

Also, don't forget to check out your local canine sporting facilities, and take the time to get you and your dog involved, because your weekend would be well spent teaching this dog how to run an Agility course, participate in a Flyball competition or retrieve floats in a dock diving contest.

In a nutshell

While learning how to choose the right puppy is important, even more important is your ability to ask and honestly answer the questions outlined in this Chapter that will help you to understand if you truly are a good fit for being the ideal guardian for the energetic Labrador.

If you don't really have the time and commitment necessary to properly socialize and raise the highly energetic Lab, you will inevitably end up with an unhappy dog, which will lead to behavioral issues, which then will lead to a stressed family, angry neighbors, and extra expenses to hire a professional to help you reverse unwanted behavioral problems.

Chapter 9: Humans Make a LOT of Stupid Mistakes

"He is your friend, your partner, your defender, your dog.
You are his life, his love, his leader.
He will be yours, faithful and true,
to the last beat of his heart.
You owe it to him to be worthy of such devotion."
— Unknown

Far too often we humans don't even realize we are the cause of creating behavioral problems in our canine companions, and when we are not aware and paying attention, we are causing a lot of issues that can actually be entirely avoided.

For instance, not taking the time to properly socialize your Labrador, forgetting about desensitizing them to loud noises, accidentally rewarding them at the wrong time, or not taking the time to teach basic rules and boundaries, can all lead to plenty of trouble in later life and create unhappiness and unwanted behavior issues.

As well, not being aware of the adolescent craziness time in a Lab's life and how to get through it, and many other less obvious mistakes, such as choosing the wrong collar or leash, sleeping in your bed, or free feeding can all result in the creation of problems.

While we humans may be well meaning, besides the obvious disasters that we can create when we don't properly train or socialize our canine friends, we can inadvertently make a lot of stupid mistakes when raising our canine companions that will cause our fur friends to needlessly suffer.

Let's begin with the more obvious *"Preventing Socialization Behavioral Issues"* that can lead to problems later in life, and proceed further into areas of *"Accidental Rewards"* that may not be so obvious, then touch upon *"Basic Rules and Boundaries"* and *"Adolescent Craziness",* and finish this chapter with *"Less Obvious Stupid Human Mistakes".*

Preventing Socialization Behavioral Issues

In order to prevent behavioral issues you first need to be aware of how easy it is to inadvertently create them yourself.

Much of how your Labrador behaves will depend entirely upon you, how extensively they were socialized as a puppy and how much they are continually being socialized throughout their life. Without proper socialization, even the most naturally friendly dog can become neurotic, unsociable and learn to act out aggressively toward unknown dogs or people.

Many people don't realize how important it is to properly and continually socialize their dogs, in several different areas, because without proper socialization, many behavioral problems could become a daily occurrence.

Never make the mistake of thinking that you only need to socialize your Lab puppy during the first few months of their life and that they will then be fine for the rest of their life, because all dogs require constant socializing.

As well, once they reach adolescence, their personality can really begin to assert itself, and this is when, without constant and vigilant daily socializing and training, any aggressive or anti-social tendencies may begin to erupt.

Generally speaking, the majority of an adult dog's habits and behavioral traits will be formed between the ages of birth and one year of age. While it is even more important to introduce puppies to a wide variety of sight, sounds, smells and situations during the most formative period in their young life, which is usually their first 16 weeks, all dogs, no matter their age, need to be exposed to different people, dogs, places and unusual sights and sounds throughout their entire adult life.

Socializing With Unknown Dogs

Any dog, despite their natural personality, that is not regularly socialized may become shy, nervous or suspicious around unfamiliar or unusual dogs or circumstances, which could lead to nervous or fearful behavior, which can then lead to aggression.

Dog walks are great opportunities for your Labrador to see and possibly meet other dogs, as well as practice proper behavior when out and about.

Remember to take it slowly and never put your dog in a situation where he or she feels uncomfortable or feels forced into being around other canines. Your dog should always be given the option to walk away, with lots of space.

If you are looking to socialise a young puppy, remember to introduce him or her to the *more calm and friendlier* of dogs, because introducing your pup to a dog that may be over boisterous or not so friendly with other dogs may result in a negative experience. This negative experience at a later date may transfer to a fear of other dogs. I would suggest finding a local puppy class with around 8-10 other puppies and allowing them to socialise but with guided play.

Socializing With Unknown People

Proper socialization also means taking your Lab puppy (or dog) everywhere with you and introducing them to many different people of all ages, sizes and ethnicities, so they will learn what is normal and acceptable in their daily life.

Also important, will be getting your puppy or dog used to the noise and unpredictable actions of young children. You will want to closely supervise play, so that children are not accidentally being too rough or screaming in high-pitched voices, because this can be very frightening for a young puppy or dog that is unfamiliar with children.

Be especially careful when introducing your puppy to young children who may accidentally hurt your puppy, because you don't want your dog to become fearful of children as this could lead to aggression issues later on in life.

Environmental Socialization

It can be a BIG mistake not to take the time to introduce your Lab puppy to a wide variety of different environments, because when they are not comfortable with different sights and sounds, this could cause them possible trauma later in their adult life.

Be creative and take your puppy everywhere you can imagine when they are young, so that no matter where they travel, whether strolling along a noisy city sidewalk or beside a peaceful shoreline, they will be equally comfortable.

Do not make the mistake of only taking your puppy into areas where you live and will frequently travel, because they need to also be comfortable visiting areas you might not often visit, such as noisy construction sites, airports or a shopping area across town.

Your puppy needs to see all sorts of sights, sounds and situations so that they will not become fearful, should they need to travel with you outside of their immediate neighbourhood.

Your Lab will take their cues from you, which means that when you are calm and in control of every situation, they will learn to be the same because they will trust your lead.

For instance, take them to the airport where they can watch people and hear planes landing and taking off, or take them to a local park where they can see a baseball game, or for a stroll beside a schoolyard at recess time when noisy children are out playing, or to the local zoo or farm and let them get a close up look at horses, pigs and ducks.

Again, never think that socialization is something that only takes place when your Lab is a young puppy, as proper socialization is ongoing for your dog's entire life.

Fear of Loud Noises

Many Labradors can show extreme fear of loud noises, such as fireworks, thunderstorms or home security alarms. We humans need to learn how to either prevent this trauma in the first place or learn how to appropriately respond to a dog that is afraid of loud noises.

When you take the time to desensitize your Lab to these types of noises when they are very young, it will be much easier on them during stormy weather, holidays such as Halloween or New Year's when fireworks are often a part of the festivities, or when your fire or security alarm is activated.

Desensitization Devices: there are several ways you can help to desensitize your Lab so that they are not fearful of high-pitched alarms, and loud, popping noises, including the following:

CDs: you can purchase CD's that are a collection of unusual sounds, such as vacuums or hoovers, airplanes, sirens, smoke alarms, fireworks, people clapping hands, screaming children, and more (or you can easily make your own), that you can play while working in your kitchen or relaxing in your living room or lounge.

When you play these sounds and pretend that everything is normal, the next time your puppy or dog hears these types of sounds elsewhere, they will not become upset or agitated because they have learned to ignore them.

Bubble Wrap: is also another simple way to desensitize your Lab that is fearful of unexpected sounds. Show them the bubble wrap, pop a few of the cells and if they do not run away, give them a treat. You can start with the bubble wrap that has small, quieter cells, and then graduate them to the larger celled (louder) bubble wrap.

Thunder Shirts: some dogs will respond well to wearing a *"Thunder Shirt"*, which is specifically designed to alleviate anxiety or trauma associated with loud rumbling, popping or banging noises. The idea behind the design of the Thunder Shirt is that the gentle pressure it creates is similar to a hug that, for some dogs, has a calming effect.

Relaxation Collars: there are basically two types of collars designed to help relax or calm an upset puppy or dog. One uses scent or calming pheromones, while the other uses species-specific music at appropriate decibel levels to calm a fearful or stressed dog.

TV or Radio: sometimes all that is required to calm a Labrador that is stressed by loud noises is to play your inside TV or Radio station with the sounds of relaxing music, louder than you might normally, to help disguise the exterior noise of fireworks or thunder.

Always be aware that some dogs literally lose their minds and do things that make no sense when they hear the loud popping or screeching noises of fireworks and various alarms and start trembling, running or trying to hide and you cannot communicate with them at all.

Make certain that your dog cannot harm itself trying to escape from these types of noises, and if possible, calmly hold them until they begin to relax.

For instance, my dog, Boris, tries to escape through the drain in the bathtub (go figure) when loud popping noises make him lose his mind.

Make sure that you are acting appropriately yourself, by not panicking or having weak, *"feeling sorry"* energy around an upset dog, because this will only make matters worse; if the person who is supposed to be their support system is also feeling weak, your dog will have nowhere to turn. Instead, support them by pretending that nothing is wrong and if you must talk to them, do so in a calm, yet assertive voice.

Never underestimate the importance of taking the time to continually (not just when they are puppies) socialize and desensitize your Lab puppy to all manner of sounds, because to do so will make everyone happier in the future and will be teaching them to be a calm and well-balanced member of your family in every situation.

Accidental Rewards

Many times, we humans are accidentally rewarding our puppies and dogs for engaging in types of behavior we are not happy with, and the following are the more obvious things we are doing that are inadvertently rewarding, and thus encouraging, an unwanted behavior.

Aggression Rewards

Many people unknowingly get into the habit of accidentally rewarding their puppies or dogs for displaying nervousness, fear, barking, growling or lunging at another dog or person by picking them up, talking soothingly, or offering them a treat.

When you accidentally reward your Labrador when they are displaying unbalanced energy, this actually turns out to be a reward for them, and you will be teaching them to continue with this type of unwanted behavior.

As well, picking up a small dog or puppy when they are growling or acting out inappropriately, places them in a top dog position where they literally have just gained the higher ground.

A dog in the *"top dog"* position feels more confident and will usually then become more dominant than the person or dog they may have just growled at when they were at *"ground level"*.

Rather than accidentally rewarding your Lab for displaying unwanted behavior, the correct action to take in such a situation is to gently correct your puppy or dog with firm yet calm energy by distracting them with a *"no"*, or a quick sideways snap of the leash to get their attention back on you, so that they learn to let you deal with whatever situation has caused them to react badly.

If you allow a fearful, nervous or shy Labrador to deal with situations that unnerve them and cause them act out aggressively when they encounter unfamiliar circumstances, you will have created a problem that could escalate into something more serious.

The same is true of situations where a young puppy may feel the need to protect itself from a larger or older dog that may come charging in for a sniff or is acting confrontational. It's the human guardian's responsibility to protect their puppy, so that they do not feel that they must react with fear or aggression in order to protect themselves.

No matter the age or size of your Lab puppy or dog, allowing them to display aggression or any sort of unwanted behavior toward another dog or person is never a laughing matter and this type of behavior must be immediately curtailed.

Excitement Rewards

It's important to recognize that attention paid to an overly excited or out-of-control puppy or dog, even negative attention, is likely going to be rewarding for your fur friend. If your Lab is not receiving enough of your attention, they will quickly learn to do whatever it takes to get the attention they desire.

Bottom line, when you engage with an out-of-control puppy or dog, you end up actually rewarding them for acting out in an unstable manner, and encouraging them to continue with more overly exuberant behavior you might not be very pleased about.

Be careful that you're not teaching your Labrador to be crazy every time they see you.

For instance, chasing after a puppy when they have taken something they are not supposed to have, picking them up when they are barking or showing aggression, pushing them off when they jump on you or other people, or yelling when they refuse to come when called, are all forms of attention that can actually be rewarding and cause more of the same behavior.

Instead, stay calm and assertive and be consistent with your training, so that your Labrador learns how to control their energy and play quietly and appropriately without jumping on everyone or engaging in barking or mouthy behavior.

Interaction Rewards

If your Labrador displays excited energy simply from being petted by you, or anyone else, you will need to teach yourself, your family and your friends to ignore your fur friend until they calm down. Otherwise, you will be inadvertently teaching your canine companion that the touch of humans means excitement, and this behavioral problem will continue to escalate.

For instance, when you continue to engage with your overly excited puppy or dog, you are rewarding them for out-of-control behavior and literally teaching them that when they see humans, you want them to display excited energy.

Too many people encourage their dog to be nuts, for instance, when they return home and greet their dog in a highly excited state. While it's nice to know that your dog is happy to see you, you forget about being your dog's pack leader just a few times and this may be enough to send your dog the message that seeing humans means they must now display out-of-control excitement.

Instead, when you come home, greet your Lab calmly and quietly and if they are at all excited, do NOT touch or talk to them until they calm down. Otherwise, your dog will learn that humans are a source of excitement, and long, consistently vigilant work on your part (with help from your friends and family) will be the only way to reverse this unwanted behavior (that can be quite dangerous with bigger dogs that are around small children or unstable adults).

Another thing to keep in mind is that children are often a source of high energy and excitement that can cause a Lab puppy or dog to quickly become extremely wound up.

If you don't want to create an ongoing behavioral problem, that could accidentally get someone injured, you will need to be very vigilant about NOT permitting young children to engage with an excited Labrador.

Important Basic Rules and Boundaries

You can prevent many future behavioral problems when you take the time to ensure that your Labrador learns basic rules and boundaries. All that's necessary for effectively teaching your puppy (or dog) these basics is a calm, consistent approach, combined with your endless patience.

Basic rules and boundaries would include things such as:

- no dogs allowed in the kitchen when you are preparing food
- humans through the door first
- no sleeping in the human bed
- no drinking out of the toilet
- no raiding the garbage can or helping yourself to *"tootsie rolls"* from the cat's litter box

Many Lab puppies are ready to begin basic training at about 10 to 12 weeks of age, and some will be ready at 8 weeks. However, be careful not to overdo it when they are less than four months of age, as their attention span may be short.

With younger puppies, make your training sessions no more than 5 or 10 minutes, positive and pleasant with plenty of praise and/or treats, so that your puppy will be looking forward to their next session.

Also, begin to introduce hand signals that go along with the verbal commands so that once they learn both, you can remove the verbal commands in favor of just hand signals.

Consistently teach your puppy or dog the *All Important Three*, which is the "Come", "Sit" and "Stay" commands (more about this in Chapter 11: Training Basics For a Happy Labrador), and use them every day in every opportunity to help your young dog progress through their unpredictable adolescent period.

Adolescent Craziness

Too often, we humans become impatient and frustrated and give up on our dogs when they transition from being the cute, cuddly and mostly obedient little puppy they once were and become all kinds of craziness.

Instead of riding the adolescent storm, it is often during this confusing and trying adolescent stage of a dog's life that they end up behind bars when the humans who promised to love and protect them, abandon their once happy fur friend at the local SPCA or rescue facility.

With consistency, understanding, the right information, and endless perseverance, you and your Labrador can emerge out the other side of this adolescent period with a much stronger bond.

Firstly, you need to know that not all dogs go through an intensely crazy adolescent period. Secondly, when you remain consistent with your socializing and training during this time, you can live through puppy adolescence and come out the other side a much more knowledgeable and patient guardian.

Remember, you've already lived through potty training, teething, socializing and basic rules and boundaries with your young Lab, and you need to feel proud of all your accomplishments and the leaps and bounds you and your puppy have accomplished together over the last several months.

If your adolescent Lab is beginning to act out and push your buttons, rather than giving up on them, it's time to remain calm, consistent and persistent, and re-visit basic rules and boundaries, while keeping in mind that you will eventually be able to enjoy the happy rewards that all those months of diligent puppy training have brought to your relationship.

During adolescence, you may experience several changes in your dog's personality that you're not exactly pleased about. For instance, your young Labrador may:

- no longer be friendly with everyone
- begin to display aggressive tendencies toward other dogs
- begin to show an interest in hunting the neighbor's cat
- start to chase birds and small creatures
- dig up your back yard
- ignore you when called
- bark at everyone and every noise
- appear to have suddenly gone deaf
- raid the garbage can or counter surf
- ignore the basic commands they've already learned
- start to relieve themselves inside again
- begin to mark territory

Welcome to the world of canine adolescence, where it appears that all your previous work was for naught and your puppy has turned into some sort of monster.

Don't panic, because every dog is different and your dog's adolescent period may go by without notice. However, being prepared for the worst will help you ride any impending storm and get you both safely out the other side where you can enjoy an even closer relationship than you previously had.

The adolescent phase may be very subtle for your puppy or on the other hand, it may be so dramatic that frustration with your fur friend is becoming a daily occurrence.

If frustration is getting the upper hand, rather than letting it get worse, consider the benefits of hiring a professional, who can provide insight and valuable assistance to help you through this stage of your puppy's development.

Less Obvious Stupid Human Mistakes

There are many less obvious mistakes we humans can inadvertently make with our dogs that can also lead to behavioral problems later in life, some of which include:

Sleeping in Your Bed: many people make the mistake of allowing a crying puppy to sleep with them in their bed, and while this may help to calm and comfort a new puppy, it will set a dangerous precedent that can result in behavioral problems later in their life.

As much as it may pull on your heart strings to hear your new puppy crying the first couple of nights in their kennel, a little tough love at the beginning will keep them safe while helping them to learn to both love and respect you as their leader.

Picking Them Up at the Wrong Time: never pick your Lab puppy up if they display nervousness, fear or aggression (such as growling) toward an object, person or other pet, because this will be rewarding them for unbalanced behavior.

Instead, your puppy needs to be gently corrected by you, with firm and calm energy, so that they learn not to react with fear or aggression.

Armpit Alligators: when your Lab is a small size, be aware that many guardians get into the bad habit of carrying a small dog or puppy far too much.

Remember that they need to be on the ground and walking on their own, so that they do not become overly confident because a dog that is carried by their guardian is literally being placed in the *"top dog"* position.

Humans who constantly carry small dogs or puppies, rather than allowing them to walk on their own, can often inadvertently create what I refer to as an *"armpit alligator"* situation.

Even dogs that are friendly and not naturally wary or suspicious of strangers, can learn to become intolerant if they don't receive adequate socialization, which means that it is always possible to allow them to become protective or possessive of *"their"* humans.

Playing Too Hard or Too Long: many humans play too hard or allow their children to play too long or too roughly with their Lab puppy. You need to remember that your young puppy tires very easily and especially during the critical growing phases of their young life, they need their rest.

Hand Play: always discourage your Lab puppy from chewing or biting your hands, or any part of your body for that matter.

Do not get into the habit of playing the *"hand"* game, where you rough up your puppy and slide them across the floor with your hands, because this will teach them that your hands are playthings and you will have to work hard to break this bad habit.

When your puppy is teething, they will naturally want to chew on everything within reach, and this will include you. As cute as you might think it is, this is not an acceptable behavior and you need to gently, but firmly, discourage the habit.

A light flick with a finger on the end of your puppy nose, combined with a firm "NO" and removing the enticing fingers by making a fist when they are trying to bite human fingers, will discourage them from this activity.

Not Getting Used to Grooming: not taking the time to get your Labrador used to a regular grooming routine, including bathing, brushing, toenail clipping and teeth brushing, can lead to a lifetime of trauma for both human and dog every time these procedures must be performed.

Set aside a few minutes each day for your grooming routine.

NOTE: get your Labrador used to being up high on a table or countertop when you are grooming them. This way, when it comes time for a full grooming session or a visit to the vet's office, where they will be placed on an examination table, they will not be stressed because this will already be a familiar situation.

Free Feeding: means to keep food in your puppy's bowl 24/7, so that they can eat any time of the day or night, whenever they feel like it.

While free feeding a young puppy can be a good idea (especially with very small dogs) until they are about four or five months old, many guardians often get into the bad habit of allowing their adult dogs to continue to eat food any time they want, by leaving food out 24/7.

Getting into this type of habit can be a serious mistake, as your Labrador needs to know that you are absolutely in control of their food.

Treating Them Like Children: do not get into the bad habit of treating your Lab like a small, furry human; even though they may try their best to please you and their doggy smarts could help them to succeed in most instances, not honoring them for the amazing dog they are will only cause them confusion that could lead to behavioral problems.

IMPORTANT: remember that the one thing your Labrador is the absolute BEST at, is Being a Dog.

A well-balanced dog thrives on rules and boundaries, and when they understand that there is no question that you are their leader and they are your follower, they will live a contented, happy and stress-free life.

Distraction and Replacement: when your Lab puppy tries to chew on your hand, foot, clothing or anything else that is not fair game, you need to firmly and calmly tell them "No", and then distract them by replacing what they are not supposed to be chewing with something they are permitted to chew, such as an appropriate toy.

Make sure that you happily praise them every time they choose the toy to chew on. If your puppy persists in chewing on you, remove yourself from the equation by getting up and walking away. If they are really persistent, put them inside their kennel with a favorite chew toy until they calm down.

Always praise your puppy when they stop inappropriate behavior or replace inappropriate behavior with something that is acceptable to you, so that they begin to understand what they can and cannot do.

Flat Collar Nightmares

Many humans simply don't realize how important it is to choose the "right" kind of collar for their canine companion. Add this to the fact that there is an ever-increasing array of tempting colors and styles to choose from and it's very easy to get distracted from choosing what you really need for your dog.

What you really need in a collar is one that will also keep your Lab safe and secure. While the flat collar may be fine for a calm dog that never pulls, leaps about or suddenly tries to do an about face and take off running in a different direction to chase that teasing squirrel, this is not a very safe reality.

Of course, while you will choose what you will for your dog, after 40 some years of working with dogs and experiencing possibly every type of terrifying, unexpected disaster while out walking a dog, the ONLY collar I feel absolutely confident using (because I know my dog cannot wiggle out of it), is the "Martingale" collar.

Flat collars, unless you have them cinched up so tight that you're almost cutting off your dog's air supply, can be fairly easy for most dogs to get out of.

The Labrador is an amazing athlete, and even though you may have a firm grip on that leash, they can back away from you, wiggle, twist and contort themselves in a quick instant, flip their head and the collar is off – bye, bye doggy!

The Martingale Collar

There are several reasons why the Martingale dog collar is far superior to a flat collar:

- comfortable for your dog to wear
- safe because your dog cannot wiggle out of it
- best training collar

The Martingale collar looks much the same as a flat collar, with one very important difference – there is a triangular piece of chain in the middle of it. This chain is attached to the collar with two rings, with a third ring in the middle of the chain, which is where you attach your leash.

When there is no tension on the collar (from them pulling on the leash), the collar hangs loose and comfortable. However, when there IS tension on the collar, that little piece of chain tightens so that your dog cannot get out of their collar.

My dog has been wearing the same Martingale "training" collar for 13 years and will continue to do so, because this collar conveys important messages between my dog and myself.

That little piece of triangular chain makes a slight noise when you sharply tug it, and this sends a message to your dog that you want their attention on you. It's simply the best collar for teaching your dog to walk calmly by your side and to remind them that YOU are in charge.

When buying a Martingale collar for your Lab, take him or her with you because it needs to be the correct size to fit over the widest part of their head. Then, once you've got the right length for your dog, you need to pay strict attention to the correct way to <u>adjust</u> the collar for maximum effect and safety.

Adjusting the Martingale Collar: once you've placed the collar over your dog's head, you need to adjust the length so that when you attach the leash to the outside ring and pull it tight, when the two inside rings come together, there is still a gap between these two rings of approximately two human finger widths. You never want the two rings to touch.

You can now enjoy happy and safe walks with your Happy Labrador.

Flexi-Leash Fiasco

Personally, flexi, retractable or extendable dog leashes are high on my list of pet peeves, for several important reasons, because they:

- are dangerous for human and dog alike
- allow the dog to be in the wrong walking position
- allow the humans to forget their responsibilities
- are difficult to securely grip
- are an excuse for not properly training your dog
- can accidentally break

While many people believe that a retractable leash is a good way to allow their dogs more freedom to roam while still keeping them securely attached, the above reasons highlight why these leashes can be a very bad idea. See below for more details.

Injury to human and dog: these leashes are usually spring-loaded, many feet long (usually 26 feet or 7.9 meters), and thin cords wound up inside a cumbersome plastic compartment with a handle and a button to control how much of the leash is extended.

As you can imagine, it's far more difficult to control a Lab that is roaming about 20 or more feet away from you, than it would be if they were on a standard 4 to 6 foot leash.

Labradors are busy sniffing interesting scents and can quickly run out into traffic, be surprised by another dog rushing in or get tangled up with a person and a dog, which can cause both injury to the dogs and person, or may cause a fight between the two dogs.

These leashes are also serious tripping hazards that can cause many injuries.

For instance, the daughter of one of my dog whispering clients broke her toe as a result of tripping over a flexi-leash, I have suffered "rope" burns several times, and once was hit in the head (ouch!) with the hard and heavy plastic handle as it snapped back when the person holding it lost their grip and dropped it.

In addition, every flexi or retractable leash is equipped with a brake to stop the unwinding of the cord at various lengths. If your dog is running and all of a sudden comes to the end of their freedom, unless you drop the handle, they will be forced to come to a very abrupt stop that can injure a dog's neck or spine.

Incorrect Walking Position: the ONLY place your Lab should ever be when you're out walking is beside you, and when you allow them to freely roam 20 or more feet from wherever you are, besides being lax about teaching your dog the correct walking position, you are *"telling"* them that you are no longer in charge. A dog in charge can get you BOTH into a lot of trouble.

Forgetting Your Human Responsibilities: when you're out walking with your Lab, as their leader, you are responsible for everything they do, including picking up after them. A retractable leash allows your dog to literally be out of your sight. While we're busy chatting with a neighbor or checking your phone messages, who knows what sort of *"message"* your dog may be depositing in the neighbor's yard.

You can be fined for not picking up after your dog, not to mention gaining yourself a bad reputation from your neighbors or other more responsible dog walkers.

Difficult to Securely Grip: the flexi leash has a large, cumbersome handle that is quite slippery and difficult to securely hold onto. If your Labrador suddenly lunges or changes direction, the chances of you losing your grip are quite high, and when that happens, the consequences can be dangerously grave.

Once dropped, your dog is now dragging a bouncing, loudly clattering handle, which can be very noisy on a sidewalk or hard surface.

This very thing has happened to me in a busy, high traffic area, when walking someone else's dog, and I can tell you from first-hand experience that this is a highly stressful and frightening situation I would not want to wish on anyone.

Unless your Lab has been trained to remain calmly sitting while rifles are fired near their head, this flexi leash that seems to be chasing them can be a very scary experience.

When your dog is scared, they will run even faster, while you run after them adding to the chaos with your panic-stricken screams to stop before they get killed trying to cross a busy intersection. Not a good scene.

Poor Training: while many might believe they are giving their Labrador more freedom by using a retractable leash, they are actually missing out on properly training their dog to heel beside them and to respond appropriately to the all-important "come" or "recall" command.

The very nature of a flexi leash is such that the dog is often out in front of the person who is supposed to be in charge, and always *"pulling"*, which to an approaching dog can look like an aggressive stance, resulting in the other dog thinking he or she must retaliate with a defensive stance.

Accidental Breakage: there is a great deal of wear on a small diameter cord that is constantly unwinding and rewinding and you may not notice a worn area until it actually breaks. Then, you've got a potential runaway dog disaster to hopefully recover from before the dog gets run over by a vehicle or finds themselves in some other type of trouble.

Improve your training, have better control, make your life easier, avoid injuries, and ensure the safety and security of yourself and your furry Lab by choosing a standard 4-foot leash.

In a nutshell

It cannot be emphasized strongly enough how important it is to properly socialize your Lab puppy, and understand that we humans often unknowingly reward our dogs at the wrong time, which can actually cause behavioral issues later in life.

Re-visit the Chapter information and make sure you avoid all mistakes we humans make with our dogs, that can lead to an unhappy Labrador with behavioral problems later in life. Also, when training your puppy or dog, keep in mind that the type of leash and collar you choose can make a big difference.

Chapter 10: Happy Labrador Body Language

"Questers of the truth, that's who dogs are; seekers after the invisible scent of another being's authentic core."
— Jeffrey M. Masson

We all know good communication is not just about the words we use. Our tone of voice and our body language help to package up and deliver our meaning every day. While most people can communicate their thoughts and feelings through words, our dogs are generally reliant just on body language to let us know if they are happy or sad.

Because our dogs don't speak our language, the only way to truly comprehend and communicate with them is for us to understand and appreciate what they are telling us through their body and vocal language. Often, gestures or actions that we assume mean one thing are actually the dog telling us the exact opposite, and determining what that wagging tail or barking really means can sometimes be the difference between a belly rub and a bite.

How happy would you be if you could not communicate with your family at home? Would you develop behaviour issues with time? The obvious positive answer is also true for your beloved Lab.

They need you to understand what they are "telling you" and how they feel, in order to be a happy family member. For instance, learning to properly "read" your dog's intentions can easily prevent an unwanted encounter during a visit to the local park.

Therefore, taking the time to educate yourself about basic canine body language and paying attention to your Labrador's body language (including their face, posture, barking and tail position) is an important prerequisite for raising a content and well-behaved dog.

This Chapter will teach you exactly that; to understand what your furry friend is trying to "tell" you and how they feel, so that you can share a happy lifelong partnership together.

So, don't wait and read on.

What's With All the Wagging and Barking?

While the Labrador happily wags their tail more often and more furiously than most breeds, it can be a mistake to automatically assume that if your dog is wagging their tail, they are happy and friendly.

What Does the Wag Mean?

When determining you're a dog's true intent or demeanor, it's important to take into consideration the entire dog posture, rather than just the tail, because it's entirely possible that a dog can be wagging his or her tail just before it decides to take an aggressive lunge toward you or your dog.

More important in determining the emotional state of a Labrador is the height or positioning of their tail. For instance, a tail that is held parallel to your dog's back usually suggests that they are feeling relaxed, whereas if the tail is held stiffly vertical, this usually means that they may be feeling aggressive or dominant.

A tail held much lower can mean that your dog is feeling stressed, afraid, submissive or unwell and if the tail is tucked underneath the dog's body, this is most often a sign that the dog is feeling highly stressed, fearful or threatened by another dog or person.

Paying attention to your dog's tail can help you to know when you need to step in and make some space between your dog and another, more dominant dog.

Of course, different breeds naturally carry their tails at different heights, (and some dogs don't have tails), so you will need to take this into consideration so that you get used to their particular body language signals.

As well, the speed at which the tail is moving will give you an idea of the mental state of your dog, because the speed of the wag usually indicates how excited a dog may be.

For instance, a slow, slightly swinging wag can often mean that your Labrador is tentative about greeting another dog, and this is more of a questioning type of wag, whereas a fast-moving tail held high can mean that your dog is about to challenge or threaten another less dominant dog.

Also, a stalking stance, where your dog has raised hackles (hair along the back), lowers their head and slowly creeps forward with an intense stare often happens just before a serious attack. There is also a similar-looking *"play"* stance, and without practice, you may have difficulty identifying the difference.

I've been sworn at after politely letting a guardian of a larger dog know that their dog was stalking my smaller dog and about to do him harm, so be careful how you approach these situations and be aware.

What Does the Bark Mean?

Of course, our dogs bark for a wide variety of reasons, and every dog is different, depending upon their natural breed tendencies and how they were raised. This section discusses some of the more common reasons why a Labrador might be barking.

Communication: since the very first dog, they have communicated over long distances by howling to one another and when in closer proximity, barking to warn off other dogs approaching what they consider to be their territory, or in excitement or happiness when greeting another member of the dog pack.

Now, our domesticated Labradors have learned that barking for a wide variety of reasons, such as when alerting us to someone approaching the home, in anticipation of their favorite food, when they are afraid, frustrated or bored, or to let us know they want to play, is an effective way to get the attention of us humans because barking is a loud and difficult noise to ignore.

Danger: while our Labradors will bark to alert us to what they believe might be a dangerous situation, how do we learn to understand the difference between what our dogs perceive as danger and what is truly dangerous, or indeed how to teach our best friends the difference?

We want our dogs to tell us when there is real imminent danger and in this case, should the danger involve an unwanted intruder, we want them to bark loudly to possibly scare this threat away.

Unfortunately, many Labs are not quite as discerning as we humans might prefer, and as such they may end up barking during situations that we would consider inappropriate or just plain annoying.

When our dogs are barking for a reason we are not yet aware of, we need to calmly assess the situation rather than immediately becoming annoyed.

We also need to remember that a Labrador's sense of smell, hearing and sometimes eyesight is far more acute than our own, which means that we need to give them an opportunity to tell us if they just heard, saw or sensed something that they are worried or uncertain about.

Rather than ignoring our dogs (or yelling at them) when they are attempting to *"tell"* us that something is bothering them, even if we ourselves understand that the noise the dog just heard is only the neighbor's kids coming home from school or a postal delivery, we need to respond appropriately.

We need to calmly acknowledge our Lab's concern by saying, *"OK, good dog,"* and then ask them to come to you. This way you have quietly and calmly let your dog know that the situation is nothing to be concerned about and you have asked them to move away from the target they are concerned about, which will usually stop the barking.

Attention: many Labradors will learn to bark to get their owner's attention, just because they are bored or want to be taken outside for an interesting walk or a trip to the local park to chase a ball.

Our canine companions are very good at manipulating us in this way, and if we fall for it, we are setting up an annoying precedent that could plague us for the remainder of our relationship.

For instance, I shared my life with a Blue Heeler who would go berserk with loud barking every time we drove near a park or when we arrived at a park. Even so, I would never reward him for barking, as annoying and hard on the eardrums as it was, I had to sit calmly inside the vehicle until he stopped barking. If I had let him immediately bound out of the vehicle, I would have inadvertently taught my dog that barking got him exactly what he wanted.

When a dog is barking to gain their guardian's attention, for whatever reason, before we immediately capitulate, first we need to calmly ask our dog to do something for us. After our dog has performed a calm and quiet task for us, such as sit or lie down, then we can decide to give our dog our undivided attention.

Often you will see a dog and their guardian at the local dog park playing fetch and when the human is not throwing that ball quickly enough to satisfy the dog's desire to run and fetch, the dog will be madly barking at the guardian. This is the equivalent of being sworn at in doggy language.

Don't make the mistake of allowing your Labrador to manipulate you in this situation, because if you do, you will soon create a bad habit that will very quickly become not just annoying to you, but also annoying to everyone else at the park.

Before throwing a ball or Frisbee for a Lab that loves to retrieve, it's important to always ask the dog to sit and make eye contact with you.

Often the types of canines that are overly exuberant with chasing a ball or Frisbee have learned this barking behavior from their humans, who allowed themselves to be literally at the beck and call of their dog, and created this irritating habit by throwing the ball every time the dog barked.

In this situation, if you allow your Labrador to dictate to you when you will throw the ball, they will quickly learn that barking gets them their desired result, and you have just created an annoying, rude dog who is yelling at you in doggy language to do their bidding.

In this type of ball-retrieving scenario, the dog has become ball *"obsessed"* and is no longer really paying attention to the guardian's commands, as they are solely focusing on where the ball is.

While there are many situations in which your Lab may bark to convey a certain message (such as letting you know when they need to go outside to relieve themselves), in all other situations where the barking is done to demand attention, a toy, an object or food, this is when you need to ask them to do something for you, and then only if you want to give them what they are asking for, do you follow through.

I had a client whose Labrador would start to whine and bark as soon as he was on the phone. This was big time annoying, not to mention almost impossible to hear the person on the other end. A little dog-whispering session fixed the problem that was created by the guardian, who had permitted his dog to be the center of attention at all times and the barking was how he learned to get his guardian's attention back on him.

Bottom line, remember to stay calm when your cute Lab is demanding attention, because even negative attention can be rewarding for your dog, that can then learn further habits that will not be particularly endearing for the human side of the relationship.

Boredom or Separation Anxiety: many Labradors, especially those who have not been properly trained or that have not been allowed to understand that they have rules and boundaries, and are treated like children, will bark loudly when left at home and are bored or are feeling the anxiety of being alone.

Many times, we humans believe that our dog is barking when being left alone, because he is experiencing *"separation anxiety"*, when in fact what the dog is really experiencing is the frustration of observing a member of the pack which they believe to be their follower (i.e. You) leaving them.

This can happen when you are not a strong enough leader for your Lab and they have taken over. They may then loudly verbalize their frustration and displeasure because, in the dog world, the pack follower (you) does NOT leave the pack leader (them). *I've seen this type of situation many times over, and once the human side of the relationship steps up and takes control, it quickly reverses.*

Breaking your Lab of the habit of loud barking when they are left alone can be solved in different ways, with the most obvious being that you simply take your dog with you wherever you go, because after all, they are pack animals, and in order for them to be really happy and well balanced, they need the constant direction of their leader (which is supposed to be you).

Another much more lengthy and time consuming way to solve a barking problem, could involve hiring a professional to help assess why the problem has occurred in the first place and then devise a plan that will work for each unique situation.

Fear or Pain: another reason your adorable Labrador will bark is when they are very frightened or in pain and this is usually a type of bark that sounds quite different from all the others, often being a combination of a bark and a whine, or a yelping type of noise.

This is a bark that you will want to pay close attention to, so that you can quickly respond and offer the assistance that your dog may need.

Whatever reason your dog may be barking for, always remember that this is how they communicate and *"tell"* us that they want something or are concerned, afraid, nervous or unhappy about something, and as their guardians, we humans need to pay attention.

Raised Hackles: when your Lab approaches with raised hackles (the hair along the dog's back), while this can be an indication that the dog may be approaching with dominant or aggressive tendencies, it also may be an indication that he is excited, fearful, startled, anxious or lacks confidence.

In any of these circumstances, it's a good idea to be respectful and keep your distance until you can assess what's really going on, because even a reactive, fearful dog can quickly turn into a biting dog.

In a nutshell

Learning the Lab body language can take some time, and this Chapter will help you get started. The more you are out and about with your dog, visiting and socializing in local parks and going on walks where you will find other dogs, the more opportunity you will have to become skilled at recognizing the many subtleties of Labrador body language.

Paying attention to your Lab's verbal and body-language signals as explained above, will help you figure out what they are trying to get across to you and can make all the difference in preventing frustration for you both and raising a happy and well-behaved dog.

Chapter 11: Training Basics for a Happy Labrador

"Properly trained, a man can be dog's best friend."
— Corey Ford

It's no surprise that a properly trained Labrador will be a much happier companion that everyone enjoys being around, and will be far less likely to develop behaviour issues later in life.

When your dog respects your leadership and knows who is in charge (i.e. You), they can then relax and let you take the lead on training them, which is as it should be. Developing a basic training program and learning to teach your Lab commands and discipline is all part of starting your dog off on the right paw.

Therefore, this Chapter will focus on training basics and tips, including hand signals, as well as simple tricks that your Labrador will love to learn. You will be very happy you spent the time to learn everything contained in these pages.

All of our canine companions are amazing, natural athletes and because of this, no matter their size or breed, they need daily exercise to stay fit and healthy, so that they can be happy, and part of their exercise routine includes learning at least three training basics.

Every dog will require daily exercise to stay happy and healthy. They will love going for walks and the Labrador will especially enjoy learning routines and fun canine sports with their guardian as well as swimming, playing and socializing in a pack of other dogs.

Any type of disciplined exercise you can engage in with your Lab will help to exercise both their body and their intelligent mind and will burn off pent-up daily energy reserves, so that your dog will be a happy and contented companion that is not overweight.

If you find that your Labrador is being a pest by chewing inappropriate items around the home or being demanding of your time, or especially unruly when visitors come to call, this is likely because they are not being challenged enough or exercised often enough, or long enough each day to drain out their daily pent-up energy reserves.

A healthy, adult Labrador will thrive when being walked several times each day and will also enjoy the challenge of being engaged in other forms of disciplined activity.

The loyal, affectionate and happy Labrador is a strongly built breed of enthusiastic gun dog with a good sense of smell and a soft mouth that is highly versatile in many sporting and service areas, so use your imagination and get them involved in many sporting arenas.

This dog is patient, trusting, highly trainable and eager to please and despite their high spirited and playful nature, they can be easily trained to perform a wide variety of complicated tasks.

As an example, the highly intelligent and exceedingly versatile Labrador can be trained as a *"Sniffer Dog"* to detect illegal and harmful substances, such as arson agents, explosives, food and plants, narcotics, oil or gas leaks, toxic waste, and many other harmful substances.

This is a dog that has plenty of energy, willingness to please and a strong perseverance when they're on the job, which are qualities that make them highly valued service canines.

The Labrador can also be trained as a *"Signal Dog"* to alert hearing impaired owners to specific sounds that will keep them safe, or to be a *"Therapy Dog"* to assist those that have mobility difficulties or specific health concerns.

For instance, this clever dog can be trained to turn lights on and off, open and close doors, pick up fallen objects and return them to their owner or even pull a wheelchair.

When used in therapy situations, these highly trainable dogs are specially trained in advanced obedience and must also pass many behavior tests, so that they can assist humans in the treatment of a wide number of disorders, such as an aid to the blind.

As well, since the Labrador has a long and distinguished history as a retrieving gun dog, they can also be trained to be a superior *"SAR Dog"* (Search And Rescue). They have a really good sense of smell, are focused and energetic and can much more effectively cover large areas in search of trapped humans than a walking ground crew.

Since this breed has great stamina and enthusiasm, is so eager to please and easily trained, they can also excel in a wide variety of canine sports, such as Obedience, Agility, Flyball, Dock Diving, Tracking, Field Trials, and more.

The Labrador needs fair, firm guidance and discipline from a young age, which includes rules and boundaries, so that they firmly grasp that you are the boss and the awareness of the line they cannot ever cross, and with a little assistance from a dog whisperer or trainer, this should be easily attainable even for a novice guardian.

Even at the young age of eight weeks, this smart dog is highly capable of learning anything you can teach. If you wait until they are six months old before beginning any serious training program, you could already have a headstrong problem on your hands and a young and powerful dog that may be unwilling to heed your commands.

The backbone of helping to develop a well-balanced and happy Lab is to provide them with a routine that ensures sufficient time to satisfy their particular physical and mental exercise needs, plus additional time to play, sniff and search every day.

What you can teach this intelligent canine depends entirely upon you and the time and patience you have to devote to their education. No matter what you decide to teach your dog, always train with patience, kindness and positive rewards.

All training sessions should be happy and fun-filled with plenty of food rewards and positive reinforcement, which will ensure that your dog is a happy, attentive student who looks forward to learning new commands, tricks and routines.

Lab Puppy Training Basics

First, choose a "Discipline Sound" that will be the same for every human family member. This will make it much easier for your Lab puppy to learn what they can or cannot do and will be very useful when warning your puppy before they engage in unwanted behavior or to redirect them.

The best types of sounds are short and sharp, so that you and your family members can quickly say them and so that the sound will immediately get the attention of your puppy, as you want to be able to easily interrupt them when they are about to make a mistake.

It doesn't really matter what the sound is, so long as it gets your Lab's attention and everyone in the family is consistent. A sound that is very effective in most cases is a simple *"UH"* sound that is said sharply and with emphasis.

Most puppies and dogs respond immediately to this sound and if caught in the middle of doing something they are not supposed to be doing, they will quickly stop and give you their attention or back away from what they were doing.

Next, your Lab puppy needs to learn the Three Most Important Words, which are *"Come"*, *"Sit"* and *"Stay"*. These three basic commands will ensure that your puppy remains safe in almost every circumstance.

For instance, when your puppy correctly learns the *"Come"* command, you can always quickly bring them back to your side if you should see danger approaching. Also, when you teach your puppy the *"Sit"* and *"Stay"* commands, you will be further establishing your leadership role, and a puppy that understands that their human guardian is their leader will be a safe and happy follower.

Many puppies are ready to begin training at approximately 10 to 12 weeks of age. Make your training sessions no more than 5 or 10 minutes (2 or 3 times a day), positive and pleasant with lots of praise and/or treats so that your puppy will be looking forward to their next session.

Come: while most Lab puppies will be capable of learning commands and tricks at a young age, the first and most important command you need to teach your puppy is the recall, or *"Come"* command.

Begin the *"Come"* command inside your home. Go into a larger room, such as your living room area. Place your puppy in front of you and attach their leash or a longer line to their Martingale collar, while you back away from them a few feet.

Say the command *"Come"* in an excited, happy voice and hold your arms open wide. If they do not immediately come to you, gently give a tug on the leash, so that they understand that they are supposed to move toward you. When they come to you, happily praise them and give a treat they really enjoy.

Once your puppy can accomplish a *"Come"* command almost every time inside your home, you can then graduate them to a nearby park or quiet outside area where you will repeat the process and where there are many more distractions.

You may want to purchase an extra-long, lightweight line (25 or 50 feet), so that you are always attached to your puppy and can encourage them in the right direction should they become distracted by noises, scents and other dogs. Try to choose a time of day when there will be fewer distractions while you are training.

Sit: the "Sit" and "*Stay*" commands are both easy commands to teach that will help to keep your Lab puppy safe and out of danger in almost every circumstance. Find a quiet time to teach these commands when your puppy is not overly tired.

Ask your puppy to "Sit" and if they do not yet understand the command, show them what you mean by gently squeezing with your thumb and middle finger the area across the back that joins with their back legs.

Do NOT just push them down into a sit, as this can cause damage to their back or joints. When they sit, give them a treat and praise them.

When you say the word "*Sit*", at the same time show them the hand signal for this command. While you can use any hand signal, the universal hand signal for "*Sit*" is right arm (palm open facing upward) parallel to the floor, and then raising your arm while benting at the elbow toward your right shoulder. Once your dog is sitting reliably for you, remove the verbal "Sit" and replace it with the hand signal.

Every time you take your dog out for a walk, which is often a cause of excitement, get into the habit of asking them to sit quietly and patiently at every stage of your walk.

For instance, ask your Lab to sit and patiently wait while you put on their leash, while you put on your shoes or jacket, after you approach the door, after you are on the other side of the door, while you lock the door, every time you arrive at a street intersection or crosswalk, every time you stop during your walk to speak to a neighbor, greet a friend or admire the view, etc., and do this all in reverse when heading back home.

When you persist with the "*Sit*" training, it will soon become automatic for your Lab to calmly sit every time you stop walking. When you ask your dog to sit for you, they are learning several things all at once; that they must remain calm while paying attention to you, that you are the boss and that they must look to you for direction and respect you as their leader.

Keep in mind that a sitting Lab puppy is much more easy to control than one standing at the alert, ready to bolt out the door or jump on someone. As well, because the action of sitting helps to calm the mind of an excited puppy (or dog), teaching your puppy the *"Sit"* command is a very important part of their daily interactions with your family members as well as people you may meet when out on a walk.

When you ask your puppy to *"Sit"* before you interact in any way with them, before you go out, before you feed them, etc., you are helping to quiet their mind, while teaching them to look to you for direction, and at the same time making it more difficult for them to jump, lunge or disappear out a door.

Stay: once your puppy can reliably "Sit", say the word *"Stay"* (with authority in your voice) and hold your outstretched arm, palm open toward their head while backing away a few steps. If they try to follow, calmly say "No" and put them back into *"Sit"*. Give a treat and then say again, *"Stay"* with the hand signal and back away a few steps.

Practice these three basic *"Come"*, *"Sit"*, *"Stay"* commands everywhere you go, and use the *"Sit"* command as much as you can to ensure its success rate.

As your puppy gets older, and their attention span increases, you will be able to train for longer periods of time and introduce more complicated routines.

Hand Signals

It's really important to use the hand signals that go along with the verbal commands during training, so that once your Labrador learns both, you can remove the verbal commands in favor of just hand signals.

Hand signal training is by far the most useful and efficient training method for your Labrador. All too often we inundate our canine companions with a great deal of chatter and noise that they really don't understand, but because they are so willing to be part of our world, they soon learn the meaning of many words.

Contrary to what some people might think, the first language of a Labrador is a combination of sensing energy and watching body language, which requires no spoken word or sound.

Therefore, when we humans take the time to teach our dog hand signals for all their basic commands, we are communicating with them at a level they instinctively understand, plus we are helping them to become a focused follower, as they must watch us to understand what is required of them.

Simple Tricks

When teaching your Labrador tricks, in order to give them extra incentive, find a treat that they really like and give the treat as a positive reward and to help solidify a good performance.

Most dogs will be extra attentive during training sessions when they know that they will be rewarded with their favorite treats – especially the Labrador who is always hungry.

If your Lab is less than six months old when you begin teaching them tricks, keep your training sessions short (no more than 5 or 10 minutes) and fun. As they become adults, you can extend your sessions as they will be able to maintain their focus for longer periods of time.

Shake a Paw: who doesn't love a sweet Lab that knows how to shake a paw? This is one of the easiest tricks to teach your dog.

TIP: most dogs are naturally either right or left pawed. If you know which paw your dog favors, ask them to shake this paw. Find a quiet place to practice, without noisy distractions or other pets, and stand or sit in front of your dog. Place them in the sitting position and have a treat in your left hand.

Say the command *"Shake"* while putting your right hand behind their left or right paw and pulling the paw gently toward yourself until you are holding their paw in your hand. Immediately praise them and give them their favorite treat.

Most Labs will learn the "Shake" trick quite quickly, and very soon, once you put out your hand, your dog will immediately lift their paw and put it into your hand, without your assistance or any verbal cue.

Practice every day until they are 100% reliable with this trick, and then it will be time to add another trick to their repertoire.

Roll Over: you will find that just as your dog is naturally either right or left pawed, they will also naturally want to roll either to the right or the left side. Take advantage of this by asking your dog to roll to the side they naturally prefer.

Sit with your Labrador on the floor and put them in a lie down position. Hold a treat in your hand and place it close to their nose without allowing them to grab it. While they are in the lying position, move the treat to the right or left side of their head (the nose will follow the treat), so that they have to roll over to get to it.

You will very quickly see which side they want to naturally roll to, and once you see this, move the treat to this side. When they roll over to this side, immediately give them the treat and praise them.

You can say the verbal cue *"Over"* while you demonstrate the hand signal motion (moving your right hand in a circular motion) or moving the treat from one side of their head to the other with a half circle motion.

Sit Pretty: while this trick is a little more complicated, and most Labs pick up on it very quickly, remember that every dog is different so always exercise patience.

Find a quiet space with few distractions and sit or stand in front of your dog and ask them to *"Sit"*. Have a treat nearby (on a countertop or table) and when they sit, use both of your hands to lift up their front paws into the sitting pretty position, while saying the command *"Sit Pretty"*. Help them balance in this position, while you praise them and give them the treat.

Once your Labrador can do the balancing part of the trick quite easily without your help, sit or stand in front of your dog while asking them to *"Sit Pretty"*. Holding the treat above their head at the level of their nose would be when they sit pretty.

If they attempt to stand on their back legs to get the treat, you may be holding the treat too high, which will encourage them to stand on their back legs to reach it. Go back to the first step and put them back into the *"Sit"* position and again lift their paws while their backside remains on the floor.

Sit Pretty hand signal: hold your straight arm, fully extended, over your dog's head with a closed fist.

Make this a fun and entertaining time for both of you and practice a few times every day until they can *"Sit Pretty"* on hand signal command every time you ask.

A young puppy should be able to easily learn these basic tricks before they are six months old and when you are patient and make your training sessions short and fun for your dog, they will be eager to learn more.

Adult Training

The Labrador is an exceptionally intelligent and gifted, athletic breed that will thrive when involved in different sports and services. Therefore, in order to ensure a happy and healthy Lab that will not develop behaviour issues out of boredom or laziness, make sure that you get this dog involved in as much activity as possible, including advanced training and/or canine sports.

When your dog is a full-grown adult (approximately two years of age), you will definitely want to begin more complicated or advanced training sessions.

This is a dog that will enjoy any kind of training, and when you have the desire and patience, there is no end to the commands, tricks, routines or canine sports you can teach a happy, willing Labrador.

For instance, you may wish to teach your adult dog more advanced tricks, such as freestyle dance, or the opposite sided paw shakes or rollovers, which are more difficult than you might expect.

If you and your dog are really enjoying learning new tricks or routines together, consider teaching them a series of hand signals, such as *"Commando crawl"*, *"Speak"* or *"Jump through the human hoop"*, or perhaps get them involved in an organized canine sport.

Teaching your dog tricks and routines builds trust and respect, is fun for both of you, and a healthy way to exercise both your dog's mind and body, which will result in a happy, contented and well-behaved companion.

Over-Exercising

Be especially careful about over-exercising your Lab when really young, because their muscles and bones are not yet fully developed, and especially on hot days (carry water for them) when they can collapse from heat stroke.

Also be aware that this dog has an insatiable urge to retrieve in water, and will continue to do so even when the water is freezing cold and they are being exposed to hypothermia. Know when to stop throwing that stick or float if the water is very cold.

Playtime

Every dog needs some regular playtime each day, and while every dog will be different with respect to what types of games they may enjoy, most Labradors will really love any game involving retrieving a stick, ball, float, or Frisbee, on land or in the water.

The Labrador will also be a very excited participant in a fun game of *"Search"*, where you ask your dog to *"Sit/Stay"* while you hide a favorite treat that they then have to use their nose to find.

After a disciplined walk with your dog, they will also enjoy being given the opportunity for some off-leash freedom to really stretch out by running free to play and socialize with other similar-sized dogs at the local dog park.

In a nutshell

Taking the time to teach your highly intelligent Labrador basic rules and boundaries, plus simple tricks will keep them both mentally and physically healthy and happy and you will raise a well-behaved dog that is a joy to be around.

Always keep in mind that the Labrador is an exceptionally intelligent and gifted, *athletic* breed that will thrive when involved in different sports and activities. Therefore, in order to ensure a contented dog that will not develop behavior issues out of boredom or negligence, make sure that you get this dog to participate in as much activity as possible, including advanced training and/or canine sports.

Chapter 12: What If You Slip Up?

"The greatness of a nation and its moral progress
can be judged by the way its animals are treated."
— Mahatma Ghandi

All the information, suggestions, tips and advice given in this book is the result of more than 40 years experience helping humans positively and effectively interact with the canine world.

If you take all that is written on these pages to heart, and regularly and consistently apply them, your Labrador will be a happy family member that will not have to suffer from any behavioral issues.

However, if your lifestyle drastically changes, you forget to exercise your dog or keep on top of basic training, or you slip up for any number of reasons, problems can occur.

For instance, you may end up becoming too busy or distracted with your human life to provide your canine companion with what they need on a daily basis to be a happy and fulfilled member of your family.

Realistically, there may be any number of other reasons why you don't consistently apply the information given here, and the following is an outline of just a few of the more common behavioral issues that may occur, with some tips that may help you get back on track.

When reading the following pages, please keep in mind that a specific behavioral problem is the result of many different possibilities or circumstances that have taken place between the human individual or family and the particular dog.

This means that properly addressing a specific behavior really needs the assistance of a professional with a personal approach, who can ask the right questions to determine how the unwanted behavior occurred, because it's often not what you may have thought.

Therefore, to generically outline possible ways to reverse an unwanted behavior will be a guessing game, because without knowing the circumstances of the guardian and their family, and understanding the situation that triggered the unwanted behavior, I can only make my best guess based on previous experience with similar problems.

As an example, there might be many reasons why the Lab in question is chewing the remote control. For instance, this could be because they:

- are hungry
- are teething
- have a taste for plastic
- think the remote is a toy
- are a super high energy dog
- are left alone and are bored
- haven't been given appropriate toys to chew
- have not been taught rules and what is appropriate
- have a guardian that needs to have stronger leadership energy
- are super smart and need a job to occupy their mind
- are under-exercised
- are over-stimulated

As you can see, it's possible for almost endless scenarios and reasons why a dog may develop a particular behavioral issue.

Therefore, please understand that without much more information explaining a particular situation, the following few common behavioral problems and the suggestions for alleviating them, is my best guess.

Chewing Inappropriate Items
[Re-visit "Distraction and Replacement" in Chapter 9]

If your Lab puppy or dog is chewing the remote, your fingers, the legs of the coffee table, or any other inappropriate item(s) that are not dog toys, rather than getting upset with your dog, you need to train yourself to be much more vigilant, then distract and replace.

First make sure that all the chewing is not just because the puppy is teething. Have compassion because teething is painful for the puppy and they must chew to help alleviate the pain while those adult teeth are growing in.

Always make sure your puppy has plenty of chew toys and to help with the pain, give your puppy an old T-towel soaked in water, tied in knots and frozen in the freezer as a chew toy.

If your Labrador is a little older, already has their adult teeth and has decided that the legs on your coffee table are good chew toys, it is possible that you:

- are not paying attention and taking the time to make sure your dog receives enough daily exercise, and/or,

- you are not teaching your dog what is, and what is not, appropriate for chewing by saying a firm and convincing **"No"**, replacing the table leg with a toy they are allowed to chew, and praising them when they've got the right thing between their teeth.

Being Fearful of Loud Noises
[Re-visit *"Fear of Loud Noises"* in Chapter 9]

If you have raised a Labrador that has a fear of loud, popping noises, you have not taken the time to read this information and apply the suggestions outlined, so read it now and practice until your dog loses their fear.

Excessive Excitement When Friends Visit
[Re-visit *"Chapter 2: Overview"* and *"Chapter 11: Training Basics"*]

Make sure that you begin to teach your excitable Labrador to be a calm follower as soon as you bring them home.

Always ignore an excited dog and do not touch them until they are calm and relaxed, otherwise you will inadvertently teach them to be excited every time they see a human.

If they are overly excited when friends come to visit, stand between your dog and your friends, and create some space by pointing away and firmly telling your dog, *"GO"*, and ask your friends to ignore him or her.

Also, if you've been properly training your puppy or dog, you will have taught them to *"Sit"* on command, and a sitting dog is much more relaxed and easier to control.

Acting Aggressively on a Walk
[Re-visit *"Chapter 11: Training Basics"*]

Make sure that your Labrador is walking at your side without pulling on the leash when you are out for a walk.

When you train your dog to walk beside you, this "tells" them that YOU are their leader and in charge of every situation, which means they will be much less likely to act out. If they try to, give a sharp snap on that Martingale collar along with a strong *"NO!"* to remind them who is the boss.

Pulling When on Leash
[Re-visit *"The Martingale Collar"* in Chapter 9]

If your dog is pulling on leash, chances are he or she is not wearing the proper training collar and you have not taken the time to teach them to quietly walk at your side.

Buy your dog a Martingale collar, properly adjust it, and then the next time they try to pull ahead of you, give a sharp snap to this collar (toward yourself) and firmly say the word *"Heel"*.

Repeating this process until your Lab understands can take a few minutes or several days – be consistent and persistent until your dog gets it.

Also, turning circles and changing directions suddenly when on a leash walk will quickly help to teach your dog their proper walking position, because if they are ahead of you they are going to be stepped on or walked into.

Counter Surfing or Raiding the Garbage Can
[Re-visit "Ideal Living Conditions" in Chapter 5]

Make sure you absolutely understand that the Labrador has a strong sense of smell and a very big appetite. This dog will literally eat his or herself to death, which means you must be a vigilant guardian and make sure that you never leave any food unattended or where they can reach it.

Not Obeying Commands
[Re-visit "Chapter 11: Training Basics"]

A well-trained Labrador is one that obeys the basic *"Come/Sit/Stay"* commands. If your dog is not obeying your commands, you have not taken the time to properly train them, with the result being that they ignore you and do not respect you as their leader. Get to work right away and train your dog so that everyone will be happy.

Don't get down on yourself if you occasionally slip up and are not being as vigilant as you need to be with your dog's training and maintaining rules and boundaries.

In a nutshell

We humans have our off days, which means that we will inevitably "slip up" sometimes when raising our fur friends. What you need to remember is that there is always a solution, and it's not the end of the world, because simply re-reading the relevant chapters in this book can quickly and easily get you back on track to raising your happy and well-behaved Labrador.

Chapter 13: Conclusion and Reviews

. *"Outside of a dog, a book is a man's best friend.*
Inside of a dog, it's too dark to read."
— Groucho Marx

This book is written to help anyone thinking of sharing their life with the highly intelligent and energetic Labrador, to first understand whether or not they truly have the time, energy and lifestyle that would be compatible with raising a healthy and happy dog.

Once it's been decided that the Labrador is the right breed to share your life with, this book is teaching you how to properly care for them, which will include socializing, training and providing this dog with adequate daily exercise, the best food and a safe environment so that they can live the longest and most contented life possible.

There are already plenty of books written, and many different trainers and opinions concerning how to correct a dog that may be suffering from any number of behavioral issues. However, to my knowledge, there are no breed-specific books outlining how most, if not all, Labrador issues are unknowingly created by the dog's guardian. Therefore, this breed-specific book stands out of all other current publications, because it:

- highlights that almost all Labrador problems, both mentally and physically, are a direct result of ignorance or unwillingness on the part of the human guardian to learn what their dog truly needs

- describes in detail what the human guardian needs to understand and commit to doing on a daily basis in order to match the Labrador's needs, so that they can raise a happy, healthy and well-behaved dog that never has to experience behavioral issues.

There is much knowledge for this breed contained within the pages of this book that has been gained over some 40 years working with dogs, that will help anyone serious about raising a happy Labrador to do without having to hire a professional to help them correct any sort of future behavioral problems.

In a nutshell, this book contains what you need to raise a Happy Labrador that will never experience unwanted behaviors.

What Past Clients Have to Say

The following are a few happy reviews from some of my past dog whispering clients, who did the work required to turn their Lab into a happy and well-behaved companion. I have taught these clients how to apply some of the tips and techniques described in this book (such as how to establish yourself as the pack leader) and they easily managed to get back on track to raising a happy and well-behaved companion.

Thus, if you do not take my word for the effectiveness of the methods contained in this book, take my clients' word!!

> *"Thank you for your report and teaching me to be a pack leader ... this has worked remarkably as Drew and Sammy have responded well beyond my expectations… Drew is very calm and relaxed and our walks are very enjoyable… I want you to know that I really appreciate your help… Results have been spectacular and both dogs have evolved into superheroes and have accepted me as their pack leader and respond positively…"*
> ~ Klaus, Drew, Sammy & Max the Cat

"I just wanted to thank you again for our lesson today. You really are amazing with dogs. Tim and I learned so much from you, it's really neat to see the difference it makes in the dogs when you take control..."
~ Morgan, Tim, Grizzly, Bella & Bear

"I was at the point I was ready to give Jake away because I was so concerned about how he reacted every time someone came to the door. It was really embarrassing! Honestly, within three hours of Asia being here, Jake was a different dog. We learned how to become the pack leader and control him..."
~ Sharon, Mike & Jake

"My partner and I and our dog Rollo recently moved to Victoria from up north. Rollo, unused to city life and walking on a leash, was nervous and reactive around other dogs. Asia showed us how we need to behave so he could relax. After just one session the difference was very impressive – walks have become relaxing and enjoyable again – for all of us..."
~ Tim, Mary & Rollo

"Thank you for helping me become the guardian that Ida needs. She was a good dog to start with, now she is an incredible dog. She walks well on lead, stays in my unfenced yard, and comes when called. I am often complimented on what a well-behaved dog I have. Thanks for making it all happen..."
~ Kristiane & Ida

Published by Worldwide Information Publishing 2019

Printed in Great Britain
by Amazon

59785187R00071